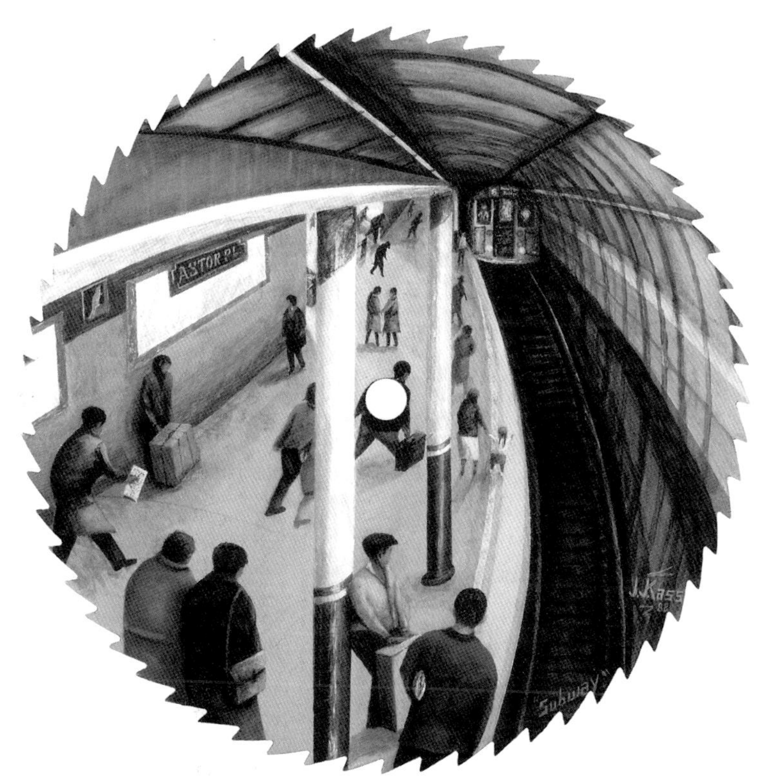
ASTOR PL.
"Subway"
J.Kass

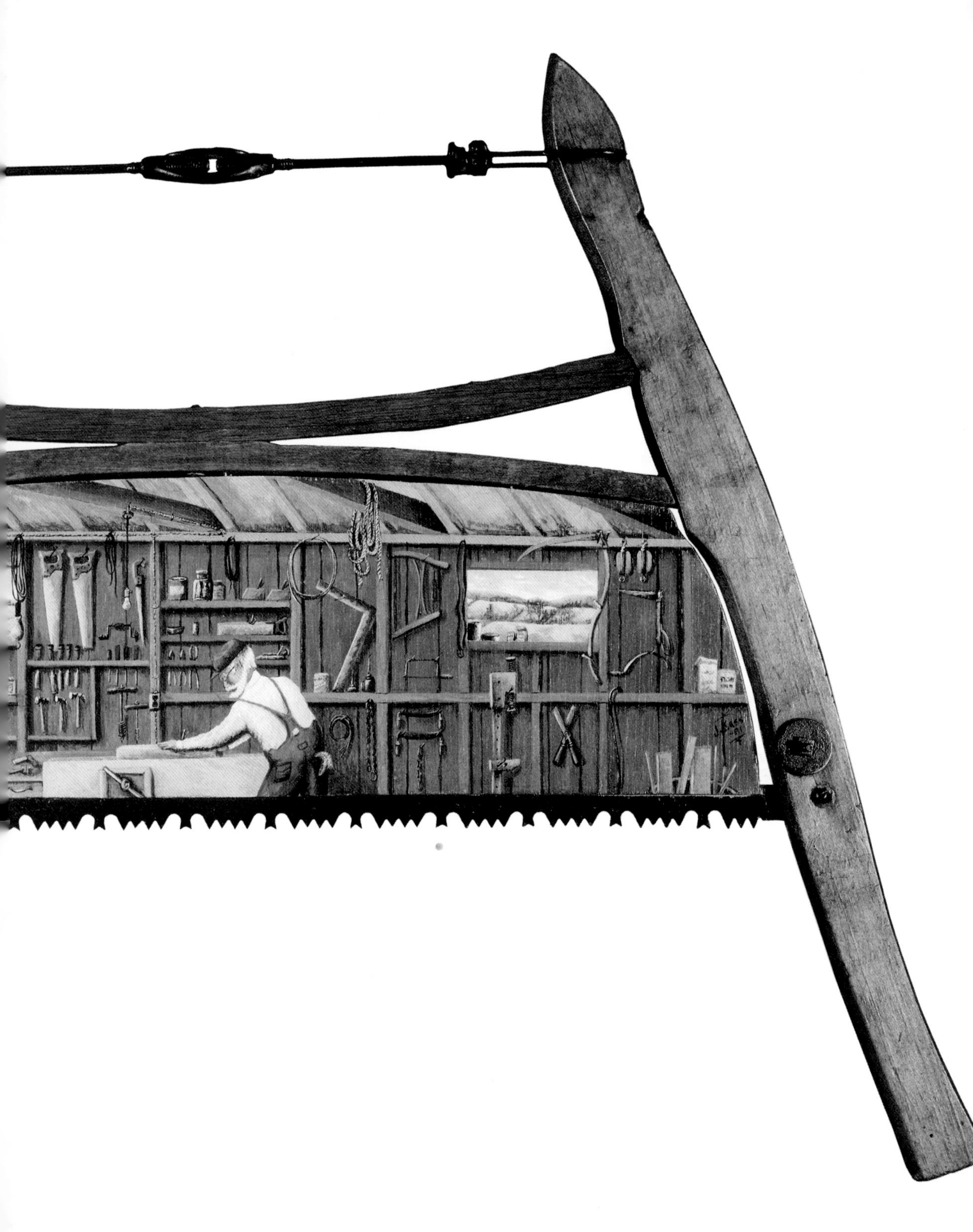

LEE KOGAN

PAINTED SAWS / JACOB KASS

AMERICAN FOLK ART MUSEUM

NEW YORK

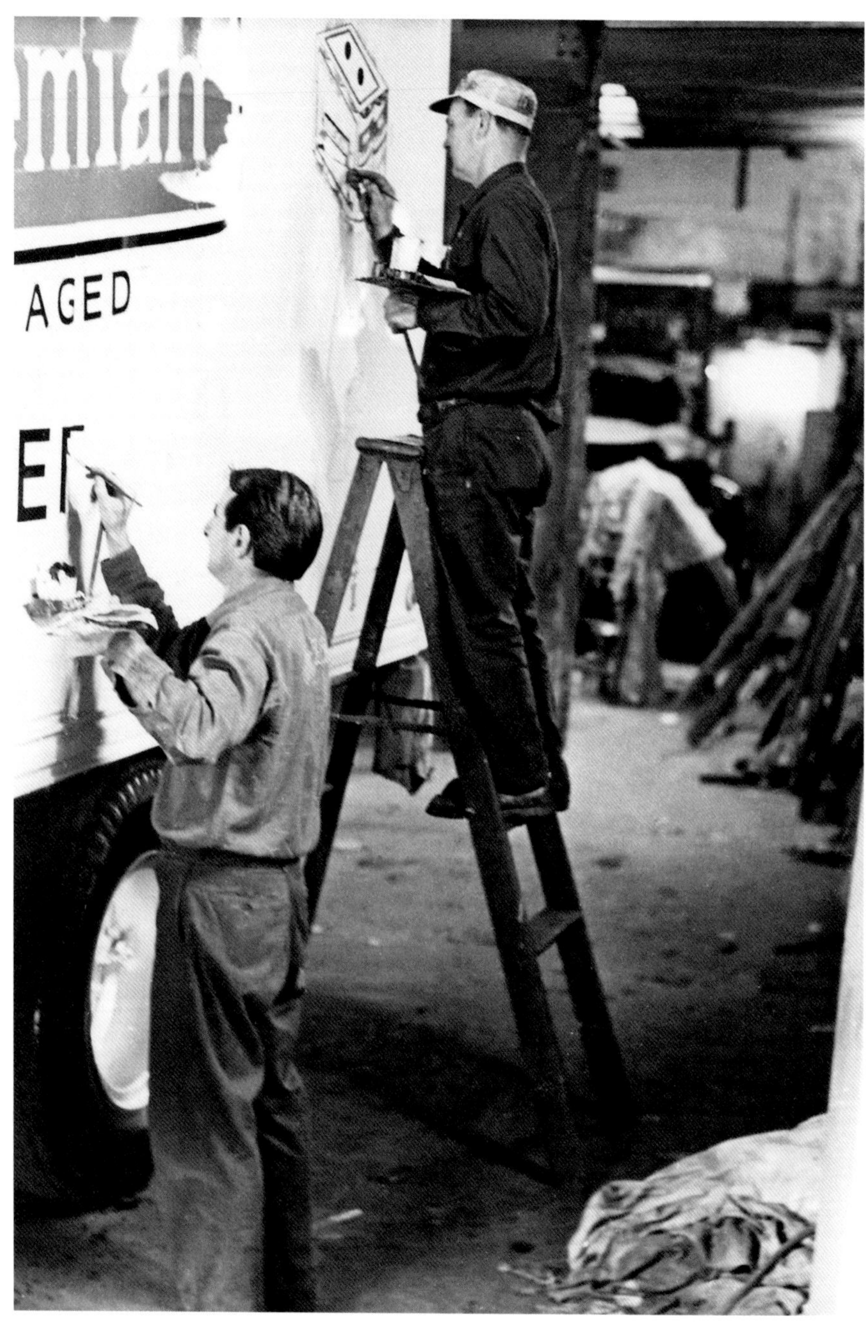

George Eagleson (left) and Jacob Kass painting an Old Bohemian beer truck, c. 1966

JACOB KASS

TRUCK PAINTER, TOOL PAINTER

Jacob J. Kass's panoramic paintings on saws and tools depict nostalgic, anecdotal scenes of American life. They are optimistic and reassuring in their sense of order, they transcend superficial sentiment, and they reflect something of the American spirit (the values of work, leisure, and community and the blessing of nature). These painted vignettes—largely benign landscapes and cityscapes—serve as poignant reminders of what appear as simpler, trouble-free times. But were they really trouble free? The images, filtered through the lens of the artist's imagination, cover the sometimes turbulent years from the early part of the twentieth century through the 1980s. Through his art, Kass—a professional truck painter, designer, and letterer long before he started painting on saws—reflected a certain bucolic and idealized image of twentieth-century America.

Jacob Kass (1910–2000) earned his living as a painter and the manager of a family business, but his satisfaction as a working artist truly began after his retirement. It is curious but natural that he chose to continue painting as a hobby following a five-decade career as a master letterer and painter of commercial vehicles in Brooklyn. "When I retired at age sixty-three," he wrote, "I didn't want to look at a paintbrush again in my life."[1] But he changed his mind after moving to Vershire, Vermont, where he became interested in repairing, decorating, and reselling furniture and accessories that he bought at yard sales and auctions. Kass's early embellishments on milk cans and frying pans soon gave way to decorations on saws and other cutting tools. Beginning with a depiction of his Vermont house, he painted on these tools landscapes and genre scenes of his bountiful New England surroundings, memories of his Brooklyn neighborhood, and idealized scenes in and around Largo, Florida, where he spent winters with his wife, Juliette.

It is ironic that Kass chose potentially dangerous tools—saws and sickles with jagged or sharp edges—as supports for his idealized world. But old saws and sickles were available at reasonable prices, and their varied shapes offered flat work surfaces and frequent asymmetry that provided compositional challenges. Kass painted on tools of all sizes and shapes—handsaws, circular saws, ice saws, coping saws, sickles, corn cutters, shingle cutters, and carpenter's squares. He also painted on wood panels sized to fit into the interior space of hacksaws and bucksaws. The blade

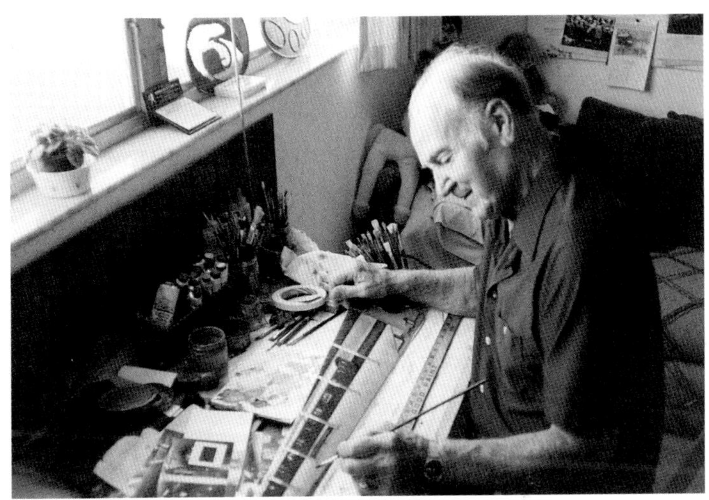

Jacob Kass in his workshop, Vershire, Vermont, mid-1980s

has potential for menace. But it also has power to harness natural forces to create a better life—in construction and agriculture, and through personal expression. Human activation of the handsaw, or "work," is at the core of Kass's paintings. Kass saw work as a basic American value; many Kass pictures focus on man at work, and he himself worked from the age of nine until his retirement. He supported his family and lent a hand when necessary to his siblings and others in the neighborhood.

The function of particular tools often sparked Kass's imagination. Hay knives hold depictions of hay gathering, while corn cutters serve as backdrops for cornfields. In *The Ice Man* (p. 48), a city scene on wood panel featuring an ice delivery is beautifully mounted within the grip of an actual ice tong, a vital part of the work. The half-section of a circular saw in *Chelsea Sawmill* (p. 23) echoes the machinery of the mill and also repeats the round shape of the logs it slices. Kass's concern for correspondence is made clear by the revelation that, mistaking a shingle cutter for a hay saw, he painted a man knifing hay on it.[2] The idea of the saw at work lends liveliness to Kass's paintings; just seeing one prompts the imagination to call up the familiar rhythmic sound of the tool in use. More concretely, the repeated jags of the saw teeth or the arc of the blade corresponds to directional movement and patterning of the rows of corn, quiltlike fields, staggered rooftops, and sleek curves of stylized urban buildings.

Unerring in their compositional strength, Kass's scenes followed the often unconventional shapes of his working surface. In *Back to the Barn* (pp. 32–33), for instance, the bucolic landscape on a slender grass sickle traces the gentle curve of the blade in a natural way. Kass's use of simultaneous perspective lends particular interest; near the blade handle, cows are seen from directly overhead, but as the eye travels along the blade surface, the view becomes frontal. In *Sawmill,* painted on a circular saw, the stream sweeps around, tracing the direction of the jagged teeth.[3] And in *Corn Cutters #1* (p. 22), the corrugated surface of a corn cutter blade is a perfect site for neatly painted, orderly rows of corn.

In the city scenes, autobiographical touches abound. Favorite subjects included Lieberman and Habacker moving trucks (see *Moving Day,* pp. 28–29)—Kass painted for Habacker for thirty-four years.[4] The handsome trucks, carefully lettered in gold leaf, were traveling advertisements (especially noticeable

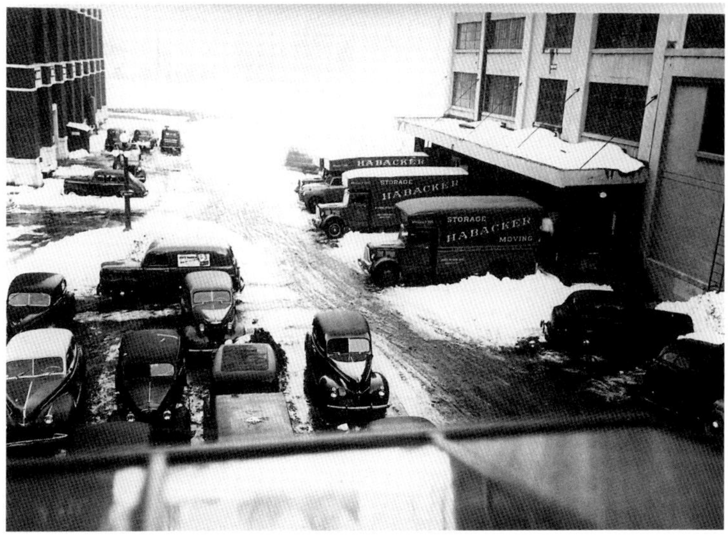

Habacker moving trucks, Brooklyn
Union Gas Company yard, Ditmas
Avenue and 83rd Street, Brooklyn,
New York, c. 1947–1949

from the 1940s on) for fleets of vans that dotted city streets
for decades.[5] Some paintings feature the pushcarts that lined
up along streets such as Blake Avenue in Brooklyn and Orchard
Street in Manhattan (see *Pushcarts,* pp. 34–35) and recall the
start-up businesses of first- and second-generation immigrant
families that settled in New York City. Subjects Kass painted
more than once include the Kass paint shop (64 Alabama
Avenue, Brooklyn), site of his father's original business, and
the subway station at Astor Place in lower Manhattan (see two
versions of *Subway,* pp. 45–47); he enjoyed the underground
bustle, people moving purposefully to and from work.

Kass's Vermont scenes likewise focus on man at work—
haying, tending the corn, cutting and storing ice for refrigera-
tion, slicing shingles for building. *My Sugar House Workshop* (p. 26)

features an older man engaged at his workbench near a wall of neatly hanging tools. He was also interested in recreation and leisure activities. He observed children in Brooklyn's East New York neighborhood playing sandlot baseball in *Picking a Team* (pp. 40–41) and winter games in *Snowball Fight* (p. 39). In Vermont, he painted a hockey game in *Choosing Sides* (p. 38), as well as a country auction and a barbecue, one of many he attended to benefit the local fire department. In Florida, he frequently painted fishing and boating scenes, such as *The Catch* (pp. 30–31). Most often he used even light without shading, a style typical of many self-taught artists. He painted the seasons, some night scenes—including variations of *Moonlight in Vermont* (p. 27)—and romantic atmospheric works.

Kass's fascination with tools grew from his experience as an artisan. His lettering skills are manifest in the small signature and occasional titles inscribed on the saws. He learned to prepare metal surfaces for paints and developed expertise in paint application, as proved by the continued excellent condition of his saws over time. His technical control came from years of experience using various types of paint brushes— "China bristle for priming, camel hair for finishing, and Russian bristle for varnishing."[6] His concern with precision led him to prepare detailed drawings (see pp. 29, 34–35, 42) and, in his early efforts, to use a grid to replicate his images.

A veteran collector, Kass kept files of images he clipped from newspapers, calendars, advertisements, and other popular sources. Among his files were folders of seascapes, landscapes, and city scenes. There were also envelopes filled with snapshots of rural and urban scenes that he utilized for selected details, as in *Subway* (pp. 46–47). These may have served as prompts for some of his commercial "picture work," such as the huge advertisement he painted for the roof of the nearby Trommer's Brewery (a pair of dwarfs on top of a huge beer bottle) or the ship logo he worked on for the Mayflower Moving and Storage Company.[7] Kass was impressed with the streamlined modernist aesthetic of futuristic buildings influenced by the "World of Tomorrow" theme of the 1939 World's Fair and borrowed ideas for both his commercial work and his tool paintings.

Like a great many self-taught artists, Kass began making art in earnest only after he retired. Retirement afforded him unlimited leisure for the first time in his life. His forays into popular, decorative painting on utilitarian objects drew praise from others, and some people even paid small sums of money to acquire his work. Unlike many such artists, however, Kass's post-retirement pursuits were directly related to the subject of his working life.

Wilhelm Kass, Jacob's father, arrived in the United States from Bavaria in 1887, at age eleven.[8] After working for twenty years in New York and Pennsylvania, with stints driving stakes for the tents of Buffalo Bill's traveling Wild West Show and grinding pigments in a paint factory, Wilhelm settled with his wife, Theresa, in East New York, where he held jobs as a painter and a construction worker. In 1907 Kass formed a partnership

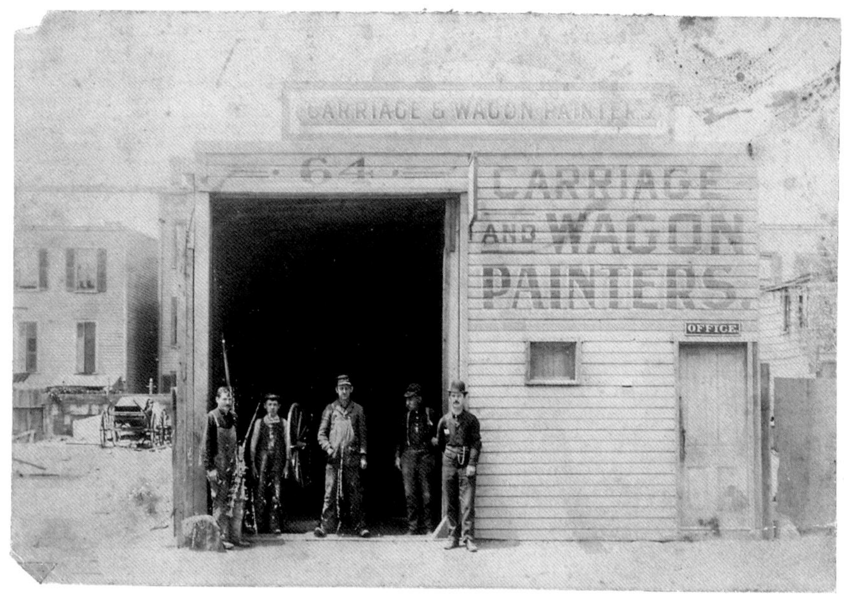

Wilhelm Kass (left)
with unidentified
workmen outside the
Kass paint shop, 1910

with William Moneypenny, a letterer, and bought a lot with a
wooden stable on Alabama Avenue a block from the Kass resi-
dence. They converted the white sidewalls to brick and lowered
the floor in the rear half by more than two feet, to accommo-
date large vans. On a small plot beside the property was a vege-
table garden, and next door were garages for a blacksmith and
mechanics.

Jacob Kass was born January 24, 1910, the last of Wilhelm
and Theresa's five children. In a 1996 interview with his son
Raymond, he described his childhood and family life as follows:

Brooklyn was covered with tenement cold-water railroad
flats that were heated with kitchen stoves. All seven of us

lived in one, until my parents bought the attached house in
Woodhaven in 1923. I went to elementary school #76 and
then #129 in East New York and later Bushwick and Rich-
mond Hill high schools until about the tenth grade, when
I left without graduating. . . .

The trolley-car barns were in East New York on Broadway and Conway Streets. There was live burlesque off
Broadway at the Gaiety and the Star theatres in the Myrtle
Avenue section of Brooklyn. . . . There were a lot of saloons
in the neighborhoods, some with swinging doors. I remem-
ber sitting with some other kids under the swinging doors
at a saloon on the corner of Liberty Avenue and Alabama
Avenue listening to the Dempsey-Firpo fight being read
from a live-action ticker tape. . . . There were popular
shopping stores on Fulton Street—A & S, Namm's,
Oppenheim & Collins, and Loeser's department stores.
Almost everyone heated with coal, and my older brothers
Willie and Charlie and I would follow the coal wagons
around the neighborhoods. . . . Some of the coal would
always spill from the chute, and we would be ready to
pick up the pieces and take it home for our stove. We
also went to the coal yard with burlap bags and picked
up the coal that would fall off the freight trains—
sometimes we would have to fight [with other boys]
to keep our booty. . . .[9]

Up to the 1930s, Jacob told Ray, William Moneypenny and Wilhelm Kass served the owners of horse-drawn wagons: moving vans, ice trucks, and beer and milk wagons.

Old timers never would learn to drive automobiles. . . . Their businesses were too small to support the acquisition of a van or truck, so they stuck to their horse-drawn wagons for a long time. . . . The average house had a stable right behind it. . . . If you did not own one, you could rent a horse for $2.00 a day. . . . When the motorized Divco trucks became the prevalent mode of transportation, every man that owned a horse had trouble letting their horse go. . . . A Divco milk truck was more efficient [because] it was stronger and faster and could carry a much bigger load, but a truck didn't help you like your horse did—for the wagon men it was a hard transition to the horseless carriage.

We had a lot of gold leaf in the old paint shop, especially on the moving vans, which were typically fancier than other types of trucks because the owners saw them as traveling advertisements. There was competition for what company had the fanciest (or gaudiest) van on the streets. Moving day was an actual event in New York in those days, and many families moved on almost a yearly basis. Gold leaf was made at Weiss Gold Leaf in a garage on Wynona Street in East New York.[10]

As a boy, he remembered, "we all worked in the paint shop
when we weren't at school, and I began helping out the letterers.
I began following Adolph Bumhardt and George Weber, one of
[Wilhelm's] earliest and best letterers. . . . [I observed Weber]
applying gold leaf to his clear varnish letters on moving vans.
Next Weber taught me pinstriping with a long sable brush and
how to put the shade accents on the letters and the fancier 'split
shades.' "[11] He practiced in his basement until he felt prepared
to work in the paint shop. Through the 1950s, Kass worked in
the shop with master letterers Weber, Charlie Kass, Bill Mansey,
and Willie Katz; through 1974 he worked with Vinnie Pucci and
George Eagleson.

Before spray painting was introduced in truck painting in
the 1930s, the designs were executed "by hand with long-haired
bristle brushes, and then sanded down with pumice, and re-
painted in successive layers—as many coats as the quality of the
job demanded."[12] Spray painting was an incredible time-saver.
The Kass shop was the largest commercial truck painting opera-
tion in New York and made "sophisticated contributions to the
refinement" of the painting process.[13] Robert Habacker recalled
that the lacquer fumes emanating from the shop in the 1950s
were very strong and that one could get a sudden high from
spending a few minutes there without a protective mask.[14]

The truck-painting artisans went beyond customary sign
painting. They memorized different styles of lettering and

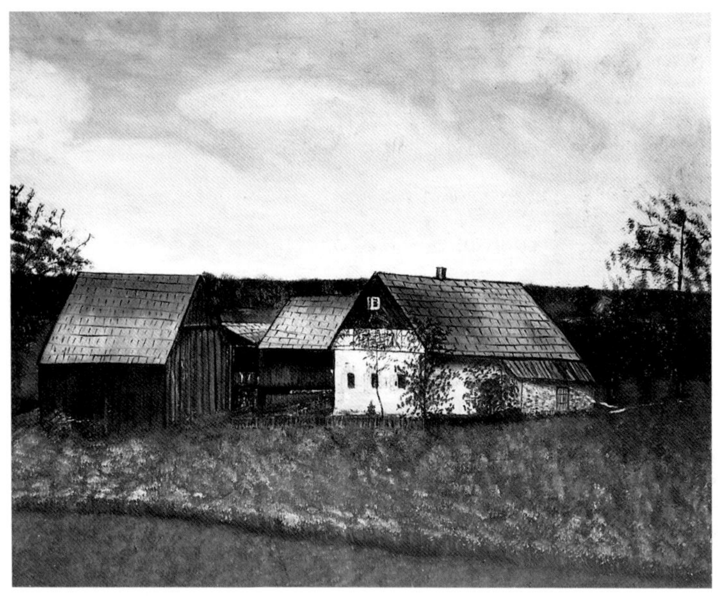

Theresa "Rose" Baier Kass Farm in Tachauer Schmettel, Bohemia, 1926, oil on wood panel, 16 × 20 in. Private collection

worked with speed and accuracy far beyond the standards of the conventional sign painter. They needed to move the freshly painted carriages, wagons, and trucks out efficiently to make room for incoming vehicles. Letterers were respected blue-collar professionals, and they were relatively well paid, like master plumbers or woodworkers. By 1946 Wm. Kass and Sons, Hooper's paint shop, and Witten Truck Painting of Bushwick dominated the Brooklyn truck-painting business.[15] Like many of his generation, Kass, who took over as head of the firm, worked excruciatingly long hours and, after paying his workers and other expenses, made only a modest profit.

Kass's interest in art was a leitmotif throughout his life. His earliest art experience was a family visit to Winkler's boarding

house in Greely, Pennsylvania, in the Pocono Mountains. During
this trip, young Jacob watched a painter create a park scene on a
stage curtain; he was impressed with the speed and deftness of
the artist's hand and with the pictorial and lettering elements.
As a teenager he copied pictures from photographs and books:
a painting of his mother's farm in Czechoslovakia, based on a
photograph, and a portrait of Sir Walter Raleigh executed on a
felt checkerboard. After he left high school, Kass signed up for
a course in commercial layout and lettering at Pratt Institute
in Brooklyn, but he left before the semester ended, believing
that he was more knowledgeable and experienced than his class-
mates were.

As a birthday present in 1939, his wife bought him Rockwell Kent's newly published *World Famous Paintings,* and that
same year Jacob copied John Constable's *The Hay Wain* (1821).[16]
When Juliette updated their home with Scandinavian furniture,
Jacob painted floor-to-ceiling murals in the house, including
a "tropical modernist" coastal scene for the dining room. This
was followed by kitchen and bedroom murals that he painted
over again and again. His son Ray, also an artist, remembers
that he and his brother, Warren, sat with their parents in front
of the television doing charcoal drawings with the popular television instructor Jon Gnagy. The elder Kass showed interest in
Ray's career as an artist but did not appreciate his son's large-
scale paintings. He occasionally sent Ray a letter with a few
drawings—"good ideas for paintings . . . to consider," with

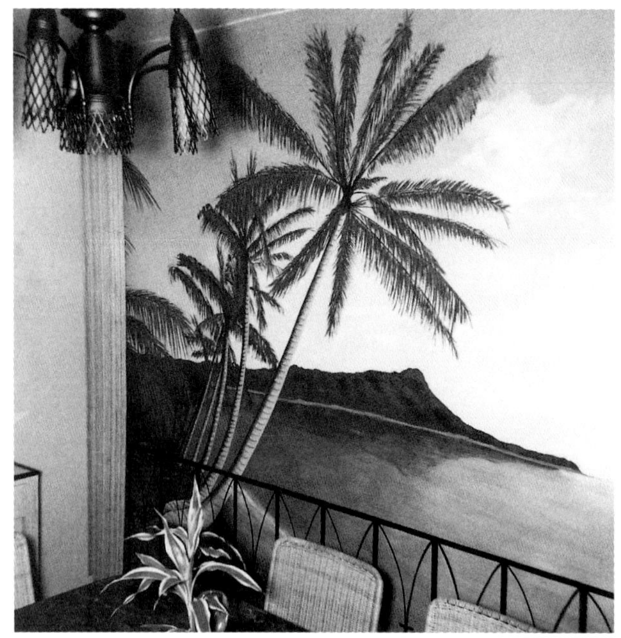

Wall mural, Kass family dining room,
Baldwin, New York, 1956

notes about "colors and blends."[17] In 1972 Ray "made a transi-
tion from a nature abstractionist to . . . landscape painter,"
and Jacob liked the resulting panoramic landscapes.[18]

In 1979 Jacob painted a saw (*Time to Rest*) for Ray's birthday. Delighted, Ray showed the saw to his agent, Allan Stone,
and asked Stone's advice on bringing his father's work to a larger
public. Stone recommended that father and son have a joint
exhibition at Stone's gallery in New York City; Jacob had exhibitions there in 1981 and 1986. In addition, solo exhibitions were
mounted at the Lowe Art Museum, University of Miami, Florida
(1982), Southeastern Center for Contemporary Art, Winston-
Salem, North Carolina (1986), Nancy Hoffman Gallery, New

York City (1987), Tampa Museum of Art, Tampa, Florida (1994),
Mennello Museum of American Folk Art, Orlando, Florida
(1999), and in the display windows of Tiffany's, New York City
(1989). In 1991 he received an individual artist grant from the
National Endowment for the Arts.

Kass's portrayals of America are broad and panoramic.
His bird's-eye scenes are reminiscent of nineteenth-century
landscapes and townscapes. Though some of his pictures seem
more intimate, he always maintains a respectful distance be-
tween himself and his subject. And yet, the smallest details are
precisely painted. His compelling painted tools have dignity and
invite the viewer to share his respect, awe, and pleasure in the
mystery of life. Kass enjoyed his life as an artist and continued
to find pleasure in painting and in the recognition it brought.
The income he received from the sale of many of his saws also
provided a more comfortable life for him and his wife: "In my
retiring years, I am fulfilling my lifelong ambition—painting
what I want to paint for the pleasure of it and not because I
have to."[19]

LEE KOGAN

Exhibition Curator

Lee Kogan is the director of the Folk Art Institute and curator of
special projects for the Contemporary Center at the American Folk
Art Museum.

1. Jacob J. Kass, "My Life and Work," in Lowe Art Museum, *Jacob J. Kass: Painted Saws* (Coral Gables, Fla.: Univ. of Miami, 1982), p. 6.

2. Raymond Kass, interview with the author, July 2001.

3. *Sawmill* (1980) is illustrated in Lowe Art Museum, *Jacob J. Kass,* p. 2.

4. Robert Habacker, telephone conversation with the author, November 10, 2001. The Charles W. Habacker Company celebrated its 100th anniversary in the trucking business in 2001.

5. In a 1970 conversation with Kass's son Ray, Willem de Kooning stated that both he and Jackson Pollock were impressed with the bright, gold leaf–lettered moving trucks that were familiar sights on city streets at the time and thought that the trucks belonged in a museum; Ray Kass, interview with the author, July 2001.

6. Kass, "My Life and Work," p. 5.

7. Kass also painted large images of zippers, lingerie, suits, cartons of eggs, and sticks of butter for various clients. His decorative painting included restoring Nunley's Carousel in Baldwin, New York (now in Syosset), and repainting the "Spirit of '76" on a horse-drawn fire wagon (private collection). This wagon was used in a background scene of the movie *Thoroughly Modern Millie* (1967); biographical notes transcribed by Ray Kass from interviews with the artist in Largo, Florida, 1996. Subsequent biographical information from notes gathered by Ray Kass, November and December 2001, with assistance from Warren Kass.

8. Ibid.

9. Ibid.

10. Ibid.

11. Ibid. Kass applied "split shades" by putting a "red or blue accent on the letter and applying a glaze made of a little black mixed with the dark glaze. To make it very fancy you then put a thin highlight on the top and right side of the letter, opposite the slit shadow on the left."

12. Ibid.

13. Ibid.

14. Robert Habacker, telephone conversation with the author, November 15, 2001.

15. Ray Kass, interview with the author, July, November, and December 2001.

16. Rockwell Kent, ed., *World Famous Paintings* (New York: Wise & Co., 1939), plate 67.

17. Ray Kass biographical notes, see note 7.

18. Ibid.

19. Kass, "My Life and Work," p. 6.

PLATES

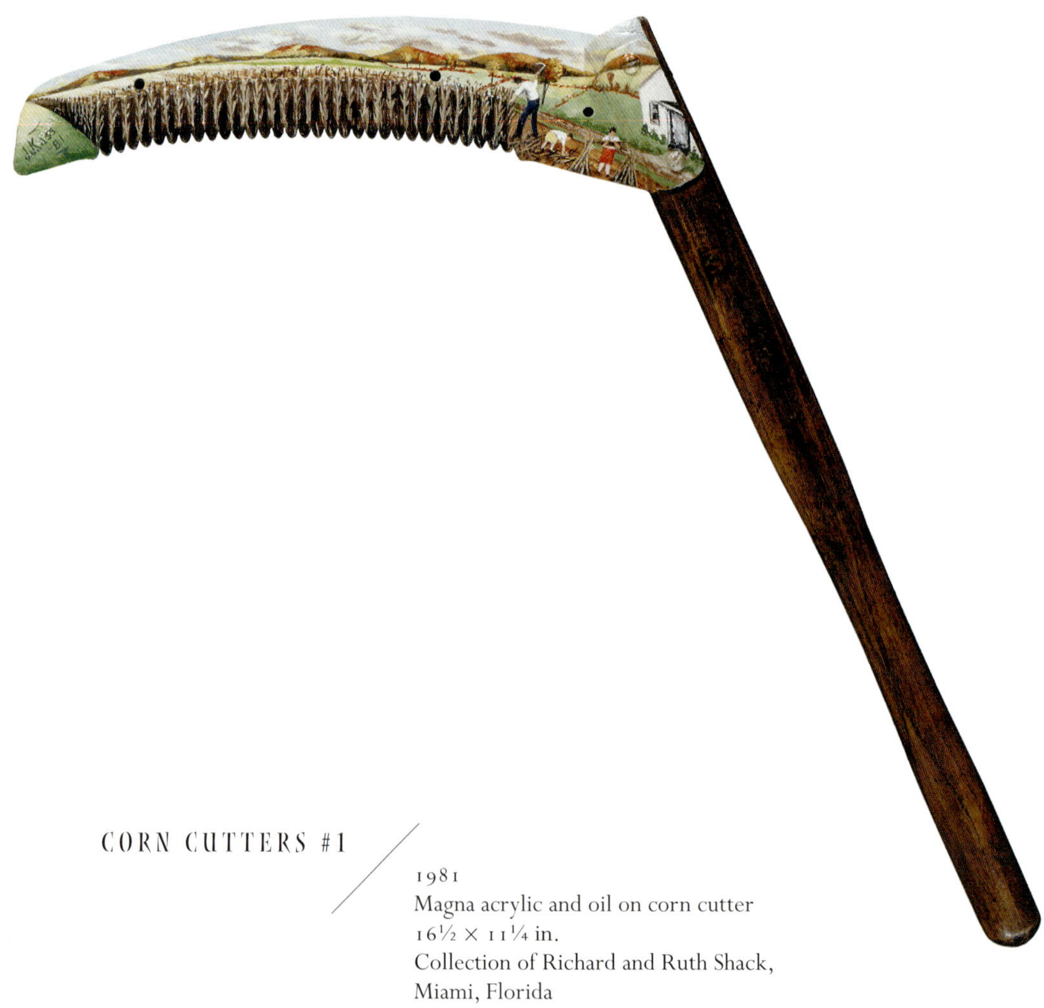

CORN CUTTERS #1

1981
Magna acrylic and oil on corn cutter
16½ × 11¼ in.
Collection of Richard and Ruth Shack,
Miami, Florida

CHELSEA SAWMILL

1980
Magna acrylic and oil on half-section
circular saw; forged iron armature
by Steven Bickley
24 × 43 × 5 in.
Private collection

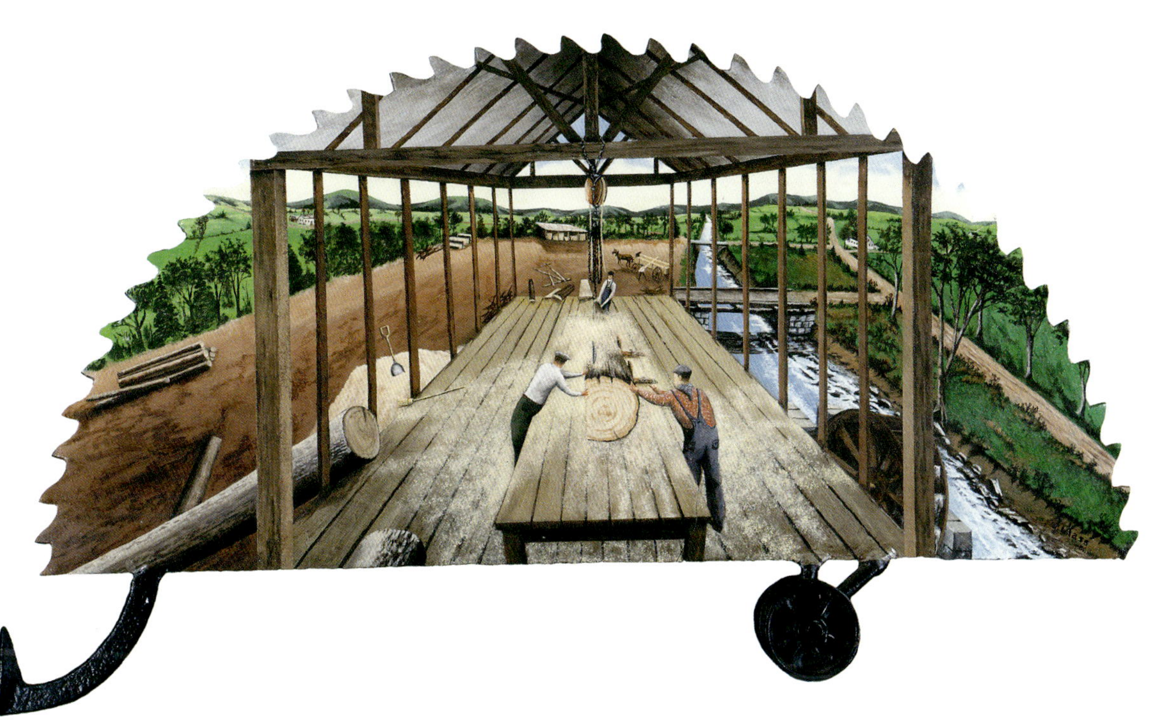

THE WHEELWRIGHT

1982
Magna acrylic and oil on draw blade
6 × 20 in.
Collection of Ivan Karp, New York

UNTITLED (HAY KNIFE)

1980
Magna acrylic and oil on hay knife
5½ × 37 in.
Collection of Nancy Hoffman,
New York

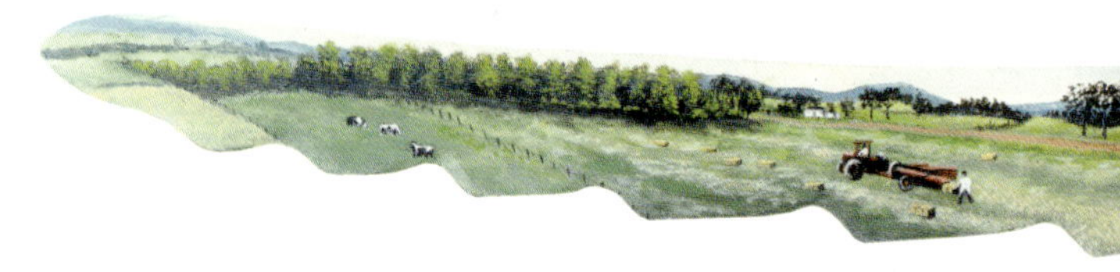

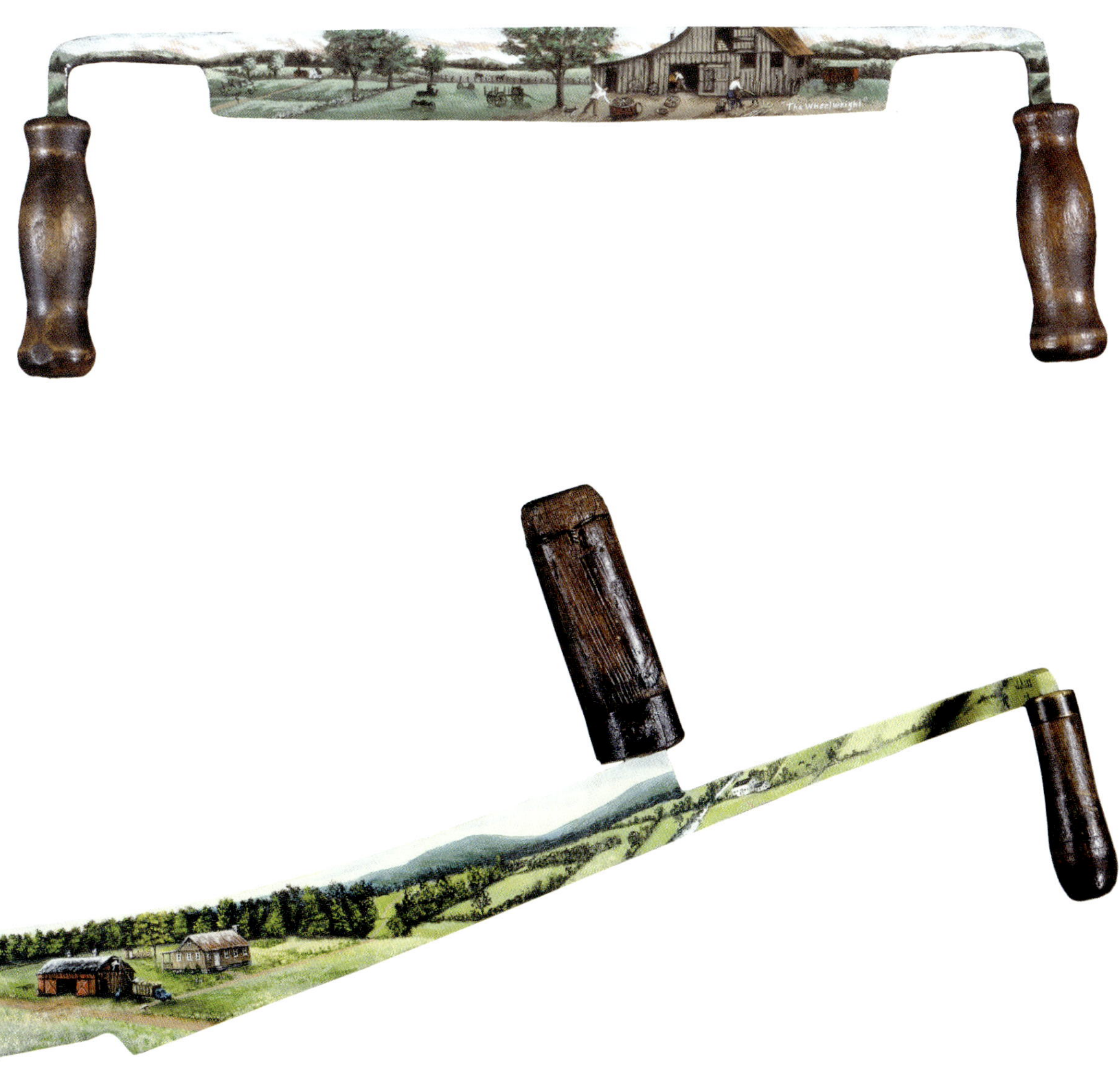
The Wheelwright

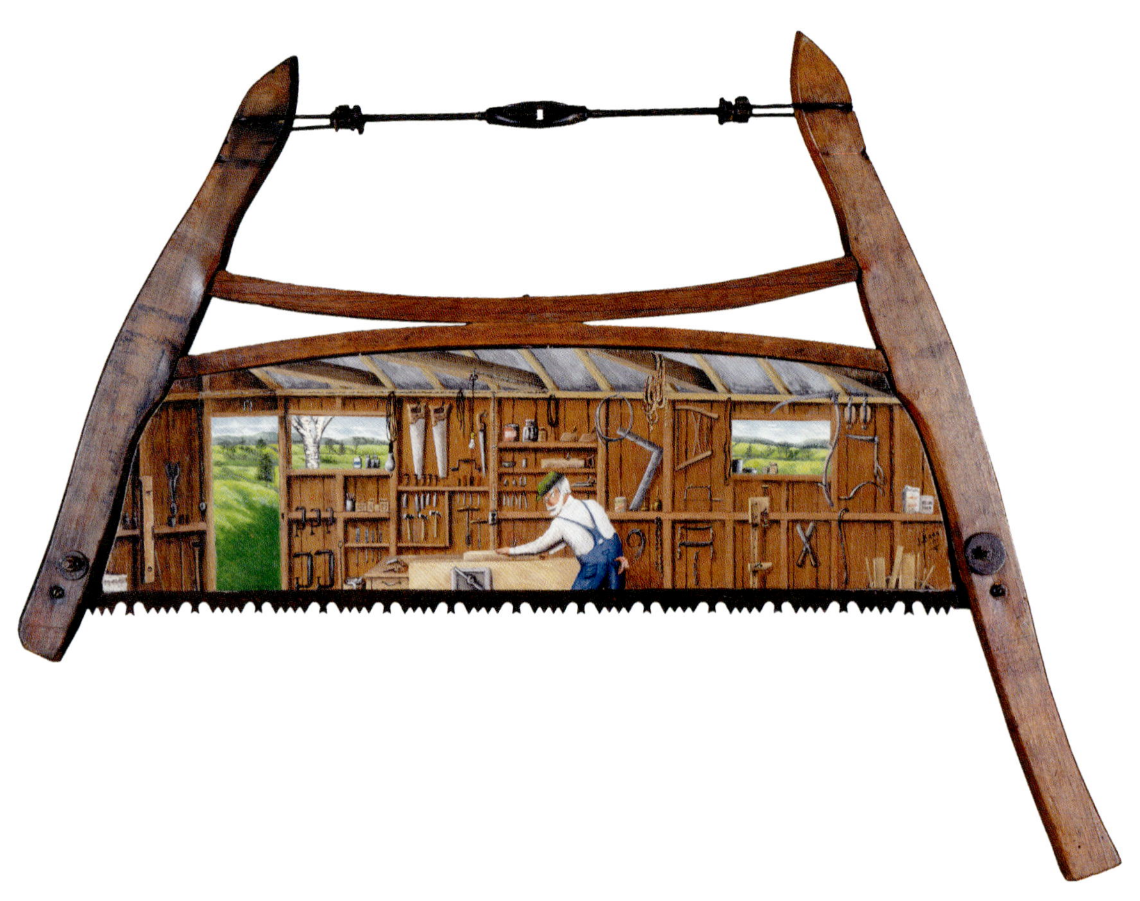

MY SUGAR HOUSE WORKSHOP

1981
Magna acrylic and oil on wood
panel mounted in bucksaw
24 × 36 in.
Private collection

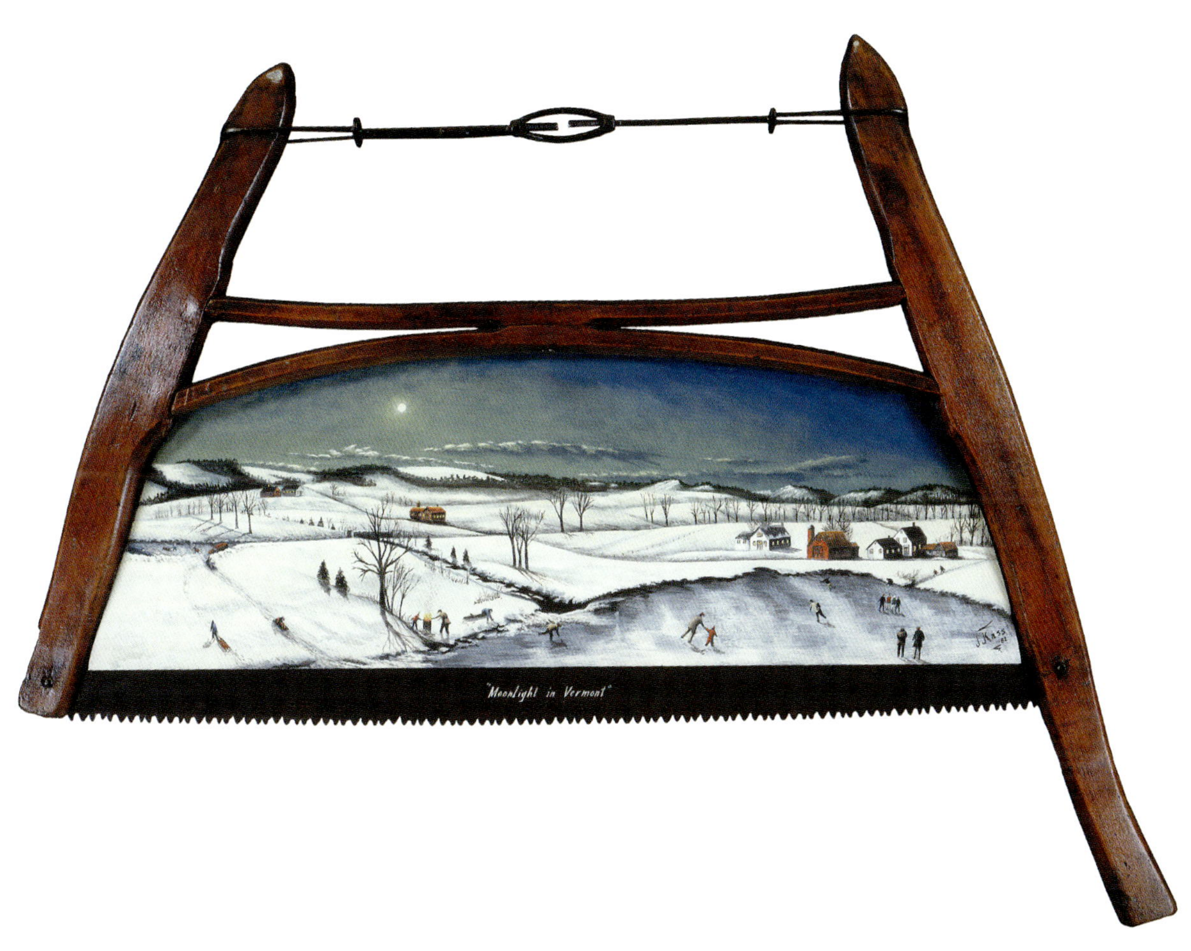

MOONLIGHT IN VERMONT #5

1982
Magna acrylic and oil on wood
panel mounted in bucksaw
26 × 33 in.
Collection of Frank Symons,
Miami, Florida

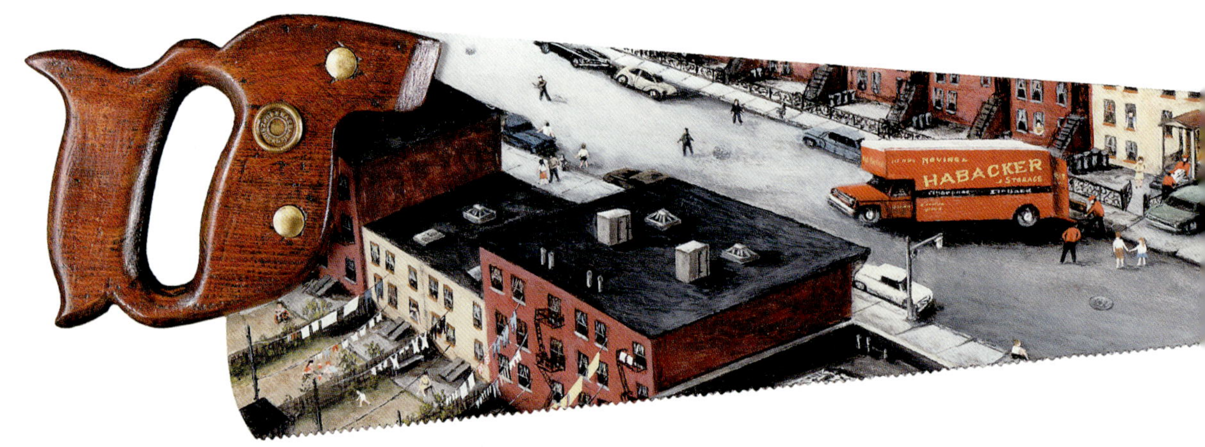

MOVING DAY

1983
Magna acrylic and oil on handsaw
6¾ × 29 in.
American Folk Art Museum, gift of
Ray Kass and Jerrie Pike, 1999.2.6

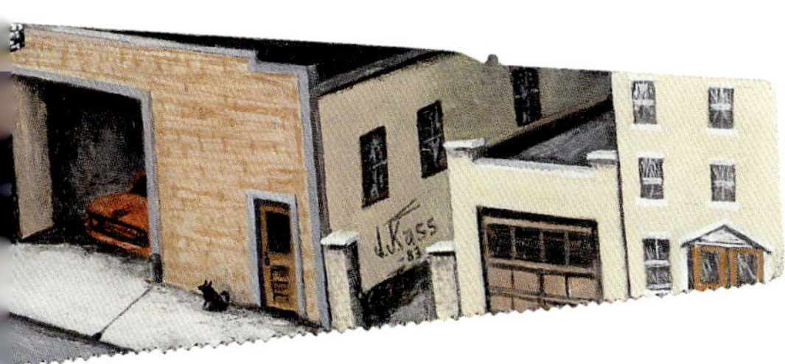

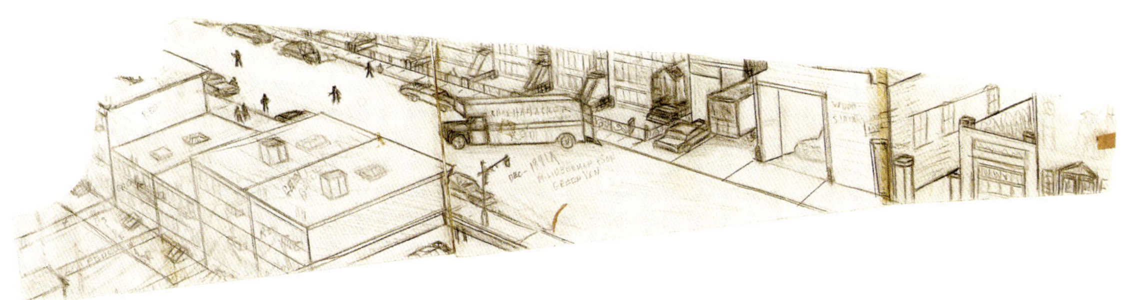

MOVING DAY #2

1982
Pencil on paper with tape
6¼ × 26¼ in.
Private collection

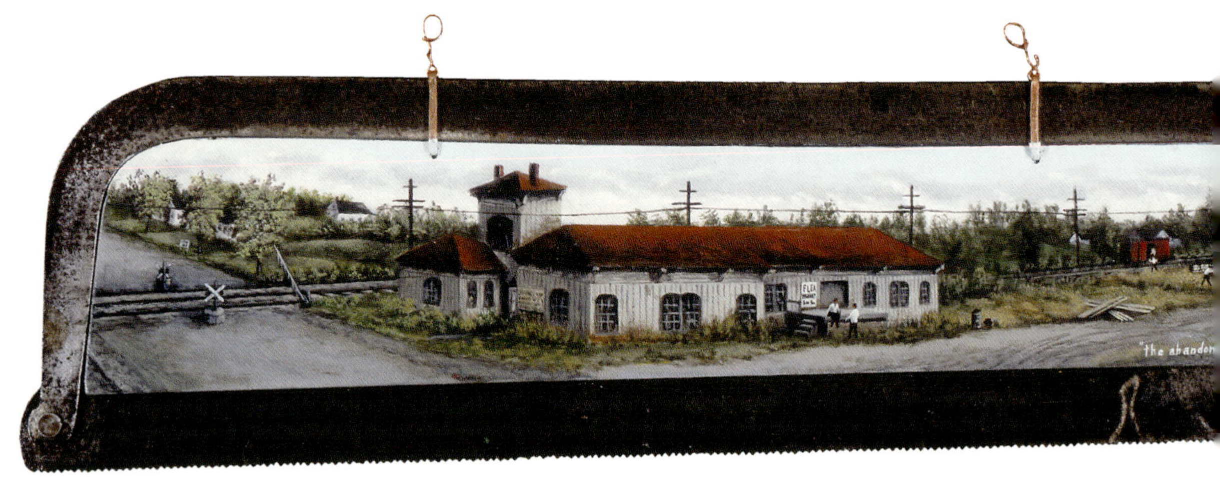

THE ABANDONED STATION

1982
Magna acrylic and oil on wood
panel mounted in hacksaw
6 × 28 in.
Collection of Nancy Hoffman
Gallery, New York

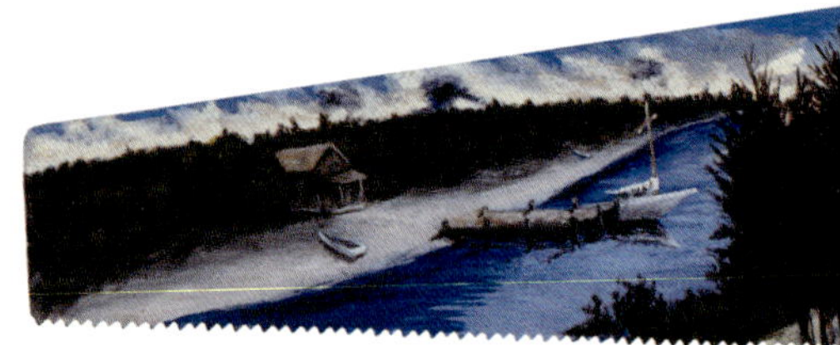

THE CATCH

1985
Magna acrylic and oil on handsaw
6¼ × 29½ in.
Tampa Museum of Art, Tampa, Florida

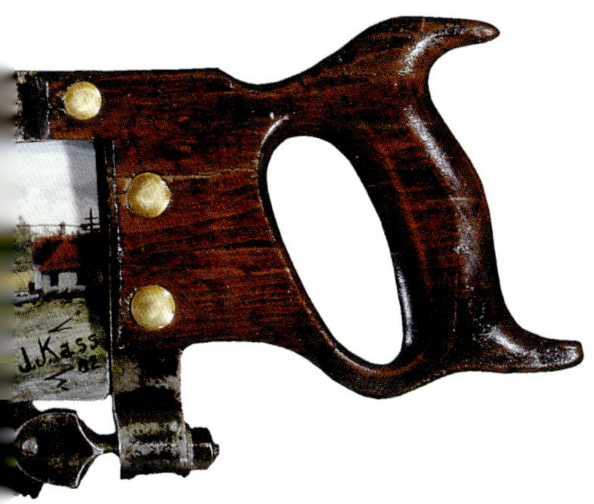

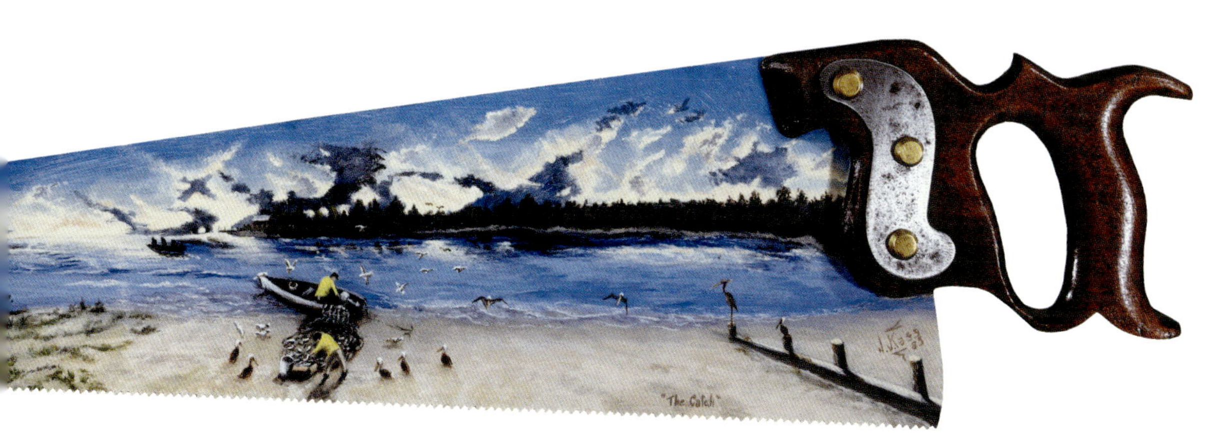

"The Catch"
J.Kass

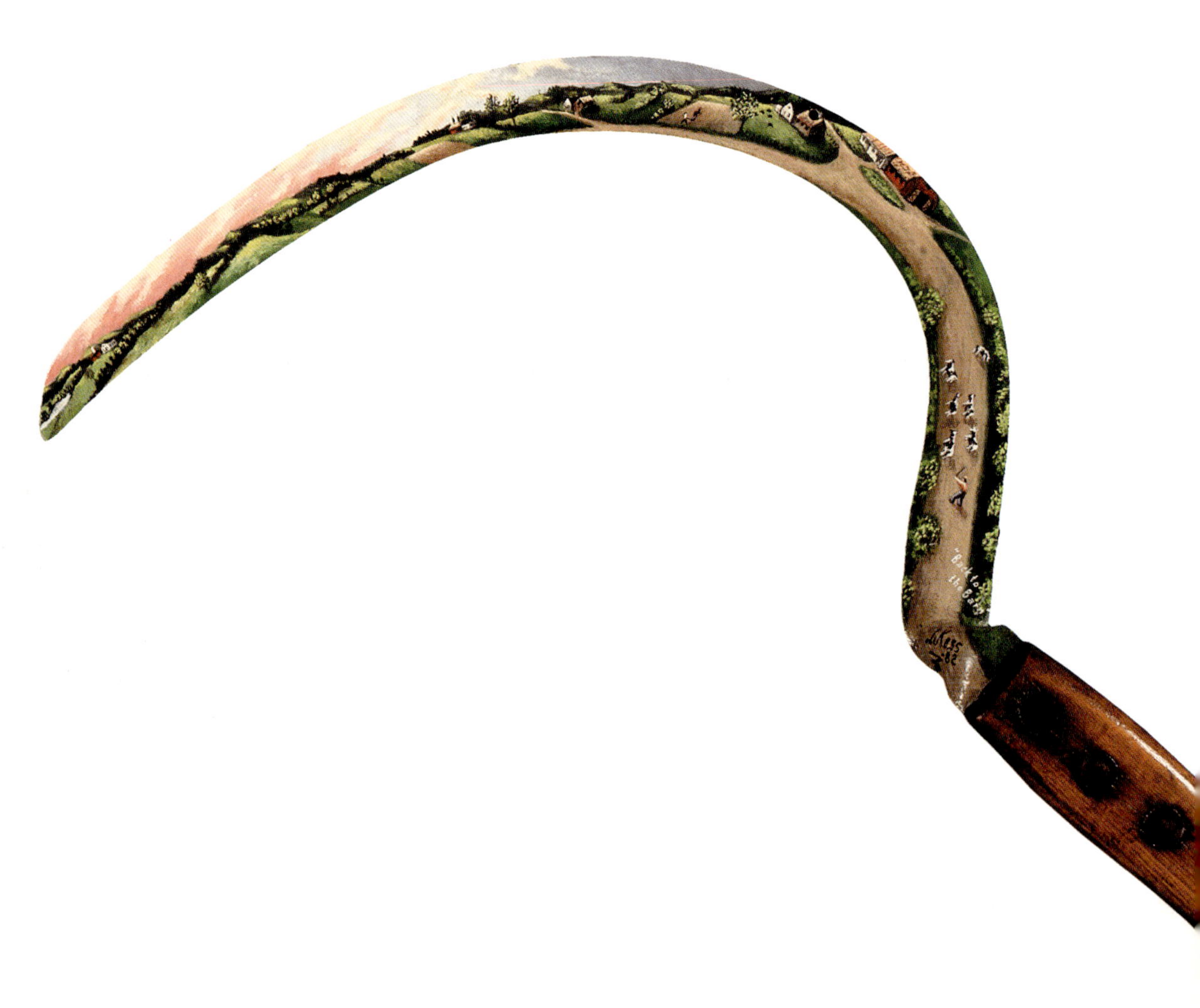

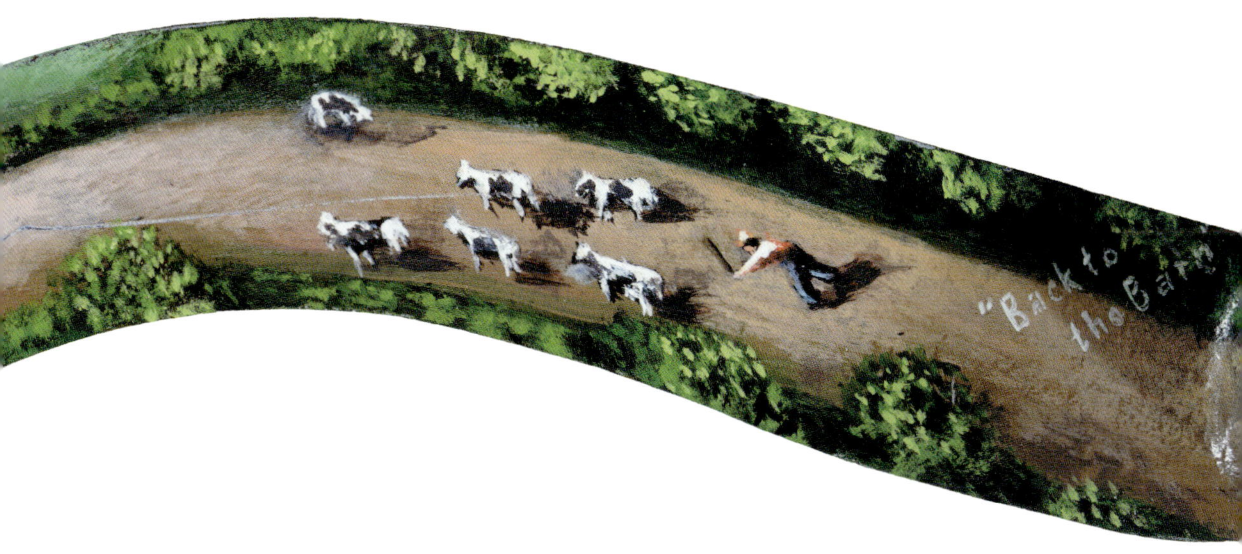

BACK TO THE BARN

1982
Magna acrylic and oil on grass sickle
$7\frac{1}{2} \times 17$ in.
Private collection

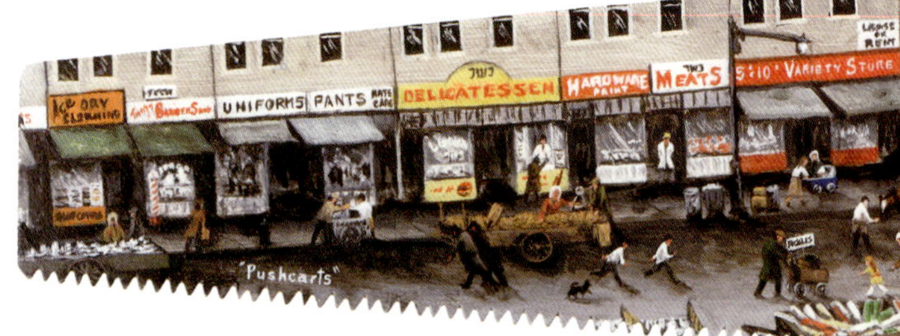

PUSHCARTS

1983
Magna acrylic and oil on handsaw
7 × 29¾ in.
American Folk Art Museum, gift of
Ray Kass and Jerrie Pike, 1999.2.7

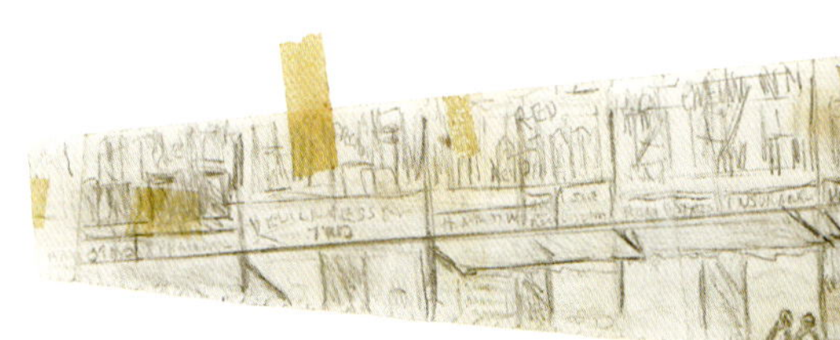

PUSHCARTS

1983
Pencil on paper with tape
6 × 26¾ in.
Private collection

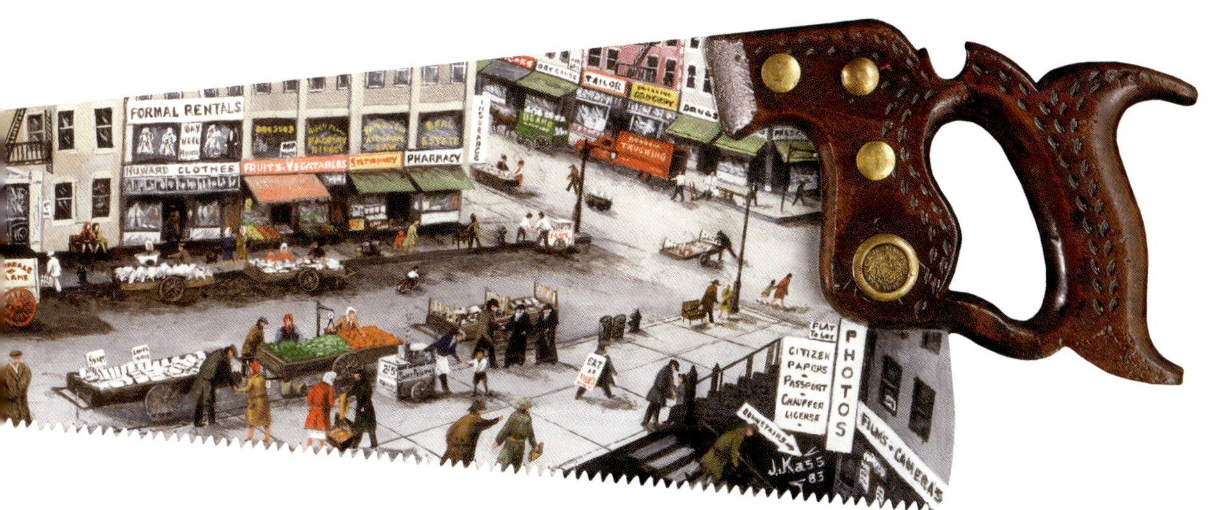
FORMAL RENTALS
HOWARD CLOTHES
FRUITS & VEGETABLES
STATIONERY
PHARMACY
TAILOR
GROCERY
DRUGS
INSURANCE
REAL ESTATE
DRESSES
CITIZEN
PAPERS
PASSPORT
CHAUFFEUR
LICENSE
FLAT
TO LET
DOWNSTAIRS
PHOTOS
FILMS · CAMERAS
J. Kass
'83

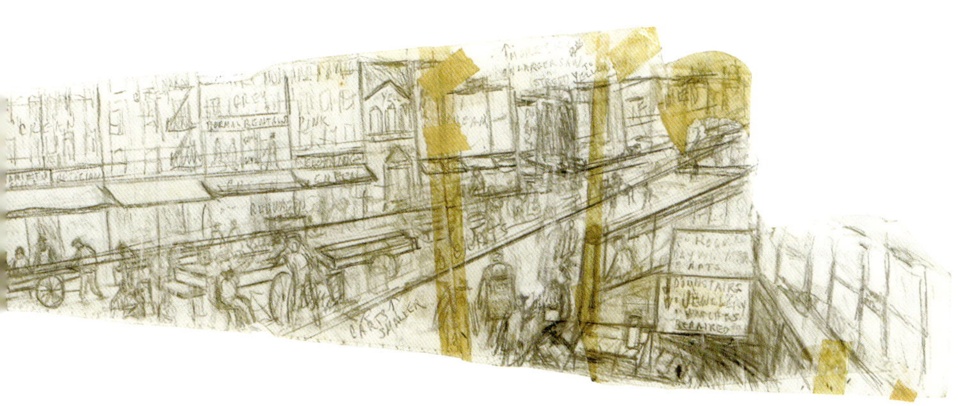
FORMAL RENTALS
PINK
CART
SHADED
DOWNSTAIRS
JEWELRY

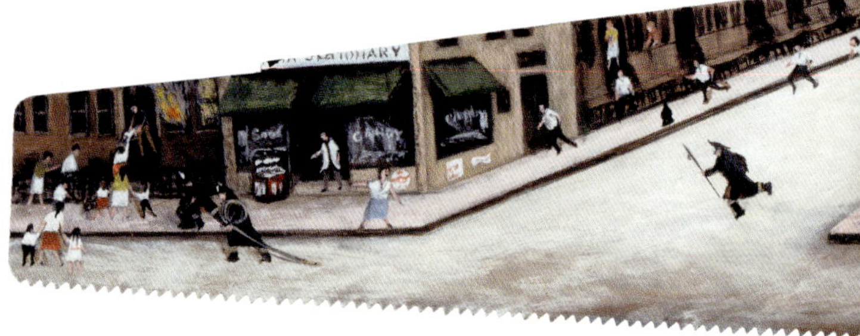

THE ALARM

1987
Magna acrylic and oil on handsaw
7 × 30⅜ in.
Collection of Thurston Twigg-Smith, Honolulu

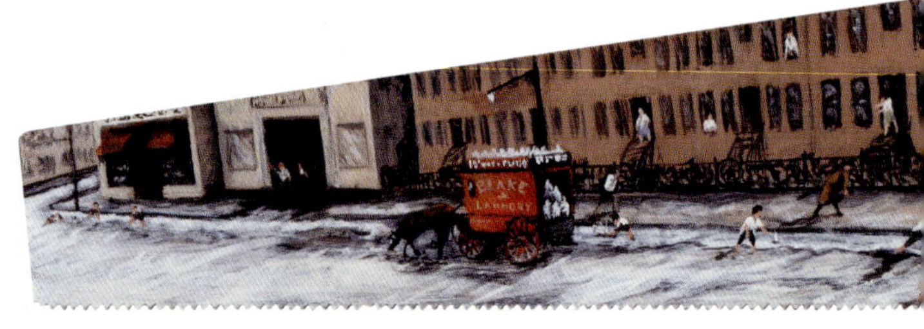

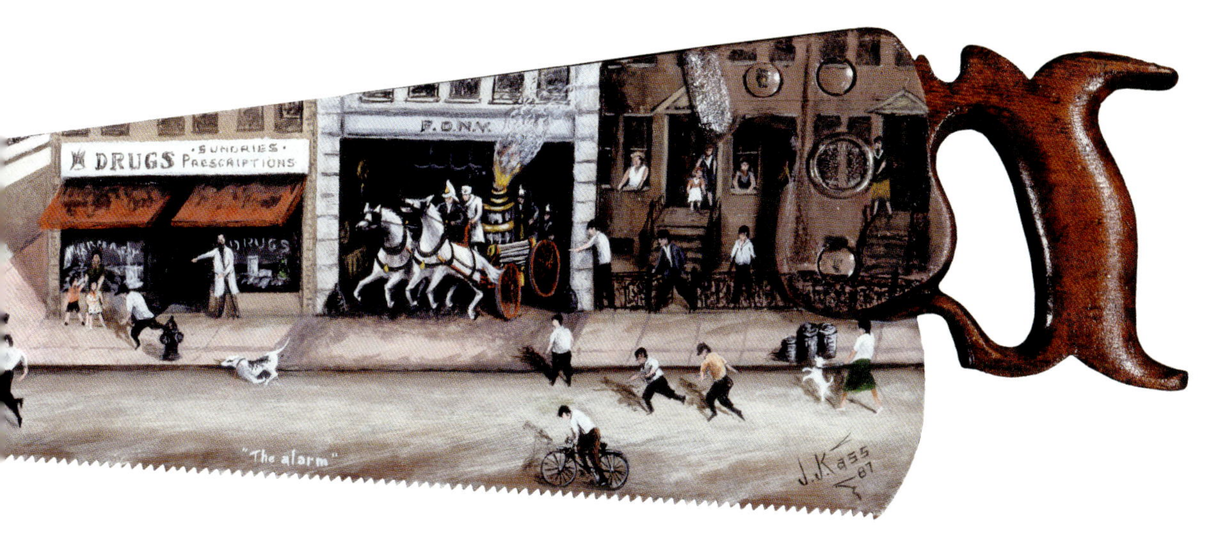

AFTER THE RAIN

1987
Magna acrylic and oil on handsaw
$5\frac{1}{2} \times 29\frac{1}{2}$ in.
Collection of Dr. and Mrs. Robert Carroll,
West Yarmouth, Massachusetts

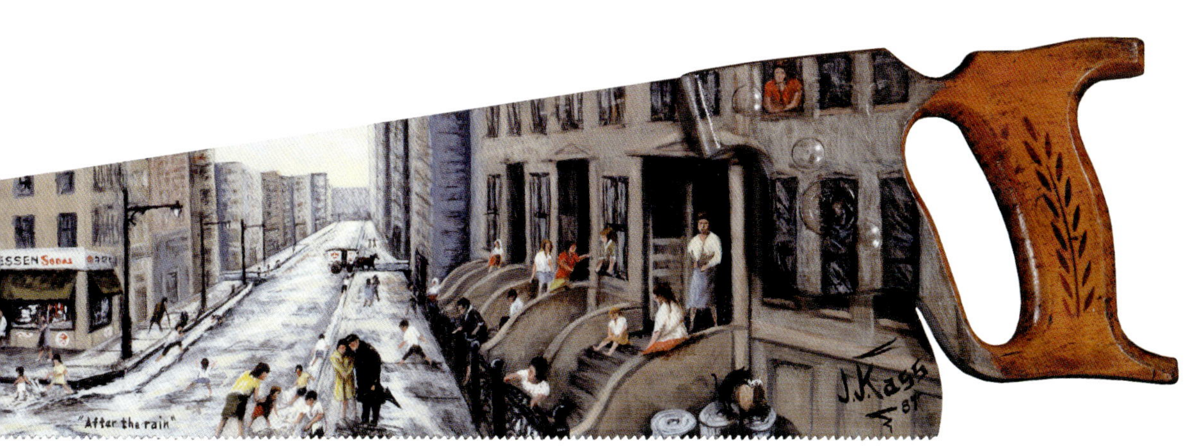

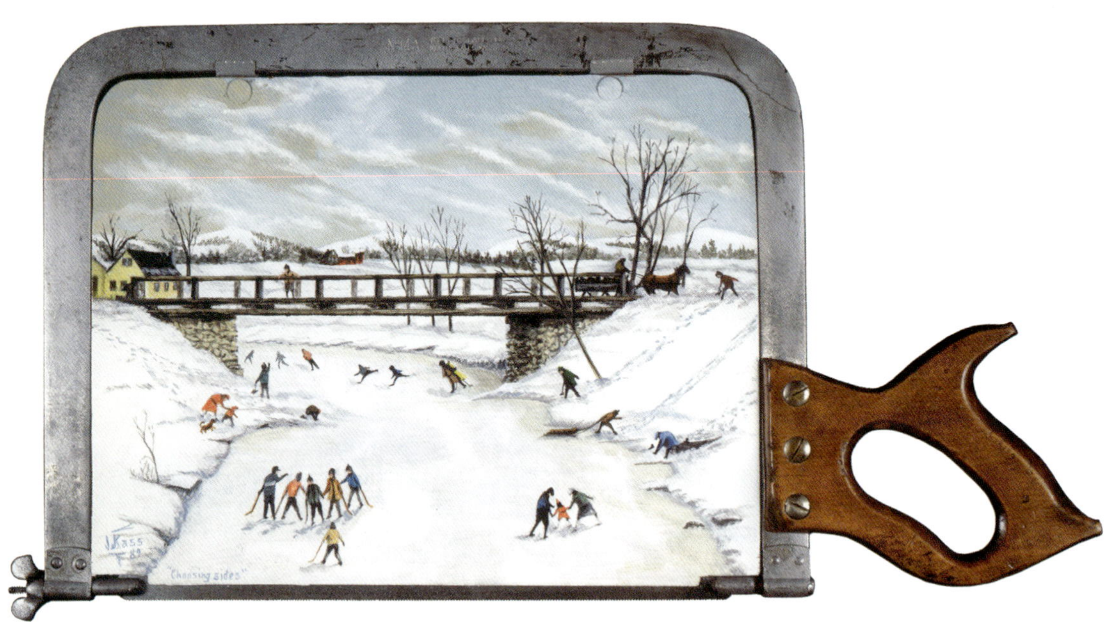

CHOOSING SIDES

1989
Magna acrylic and oil on wood
panel mounted in hacksaw
$11\frac{1}{2} \times 22$ in.
Private collection

SNOWBALL FIGHT

1988
Magna acrylic and oil on carpenter's square
$7\frac{1}{2} \times 10\frac{5}{8}$ in.
Private collection

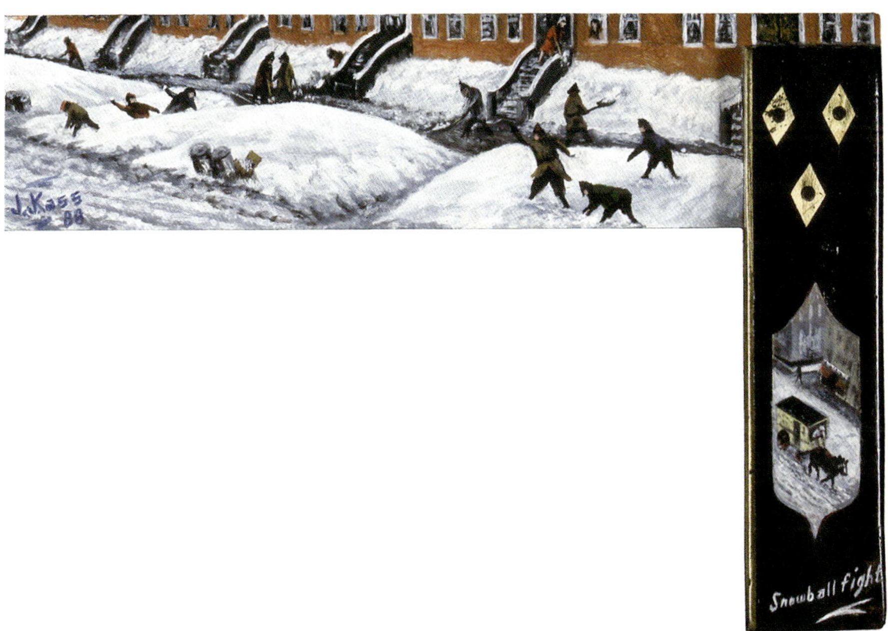

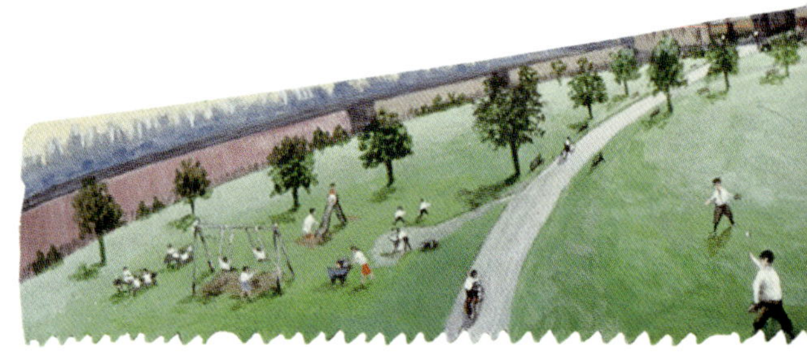

PICKING A TEAM

1985
Magna acrylic and oil on handsaw
7 × 27½ in.
Estate of Mr. and Mrs. David McCall,
New York

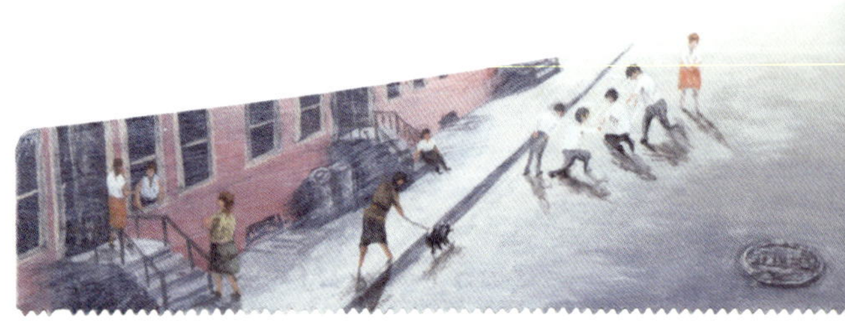

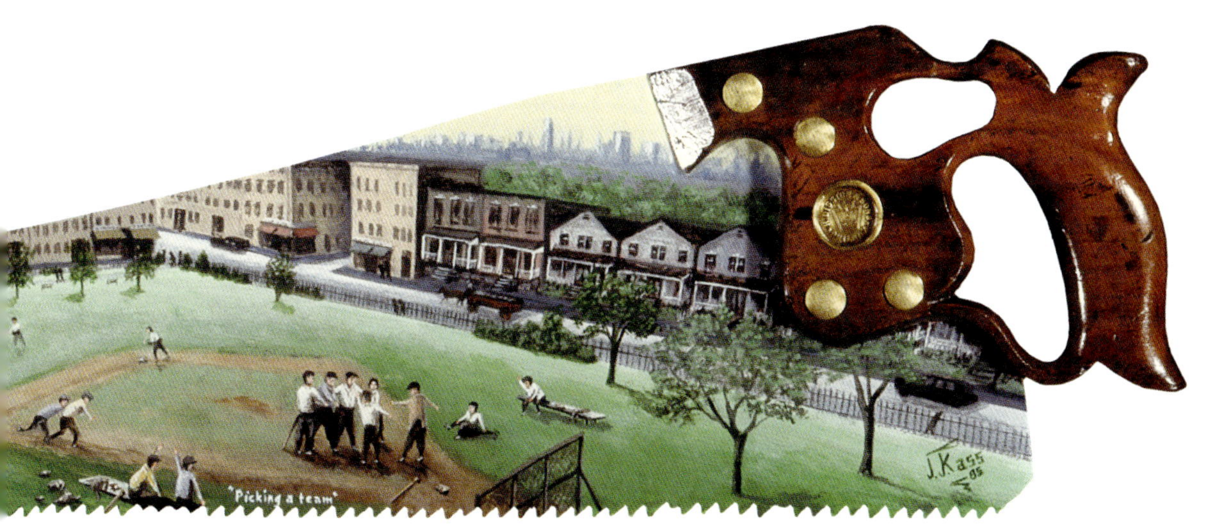

THE PAPER STAND

1987
Magna acrylic and oil on handsaw
6¾ × 28¾ in.
Collection of Lowell Schindler, courtesy
Nancy Hoffman Gallery, New York

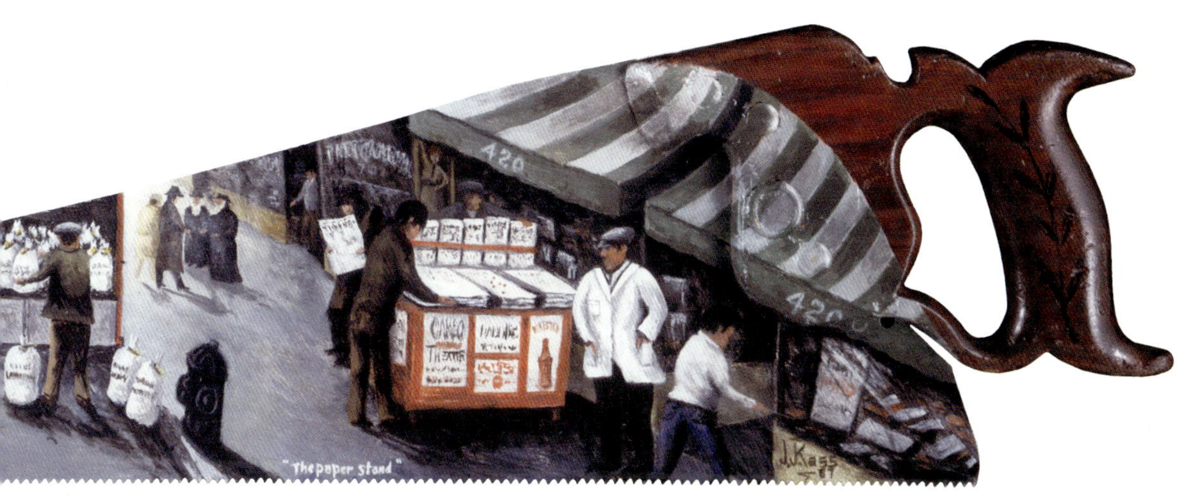

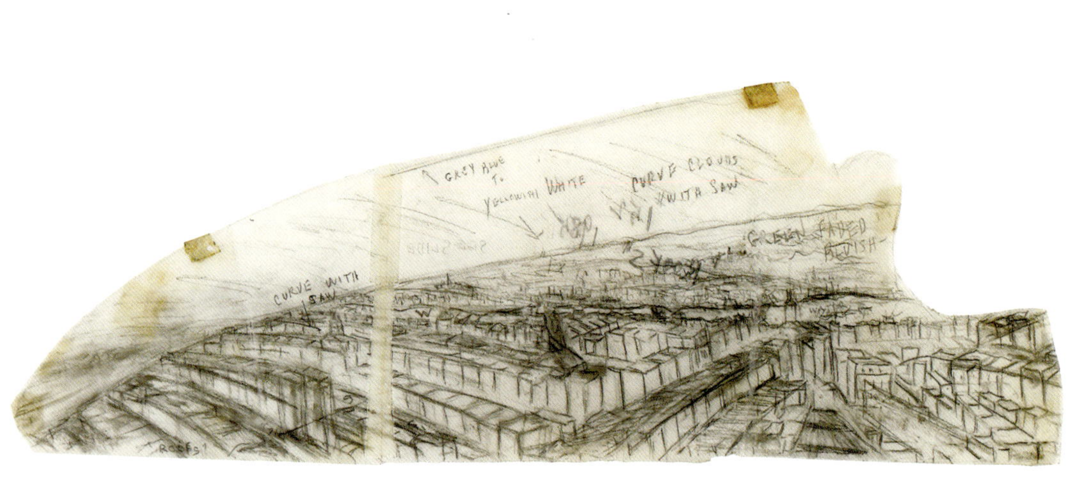

ROOFS

1985
Pencil on paper with tape
6¼ × 17¾ in.
Private collection

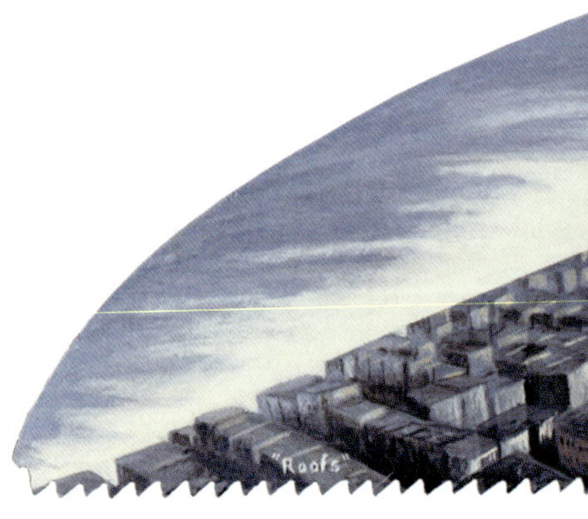

ROOFS

1985
Magna acrylic and oil on customized handsaw
7 × 21 in.
American Folk Art Museum, gift of
Ray Kass and Jerrie Pike, 1999.2.4

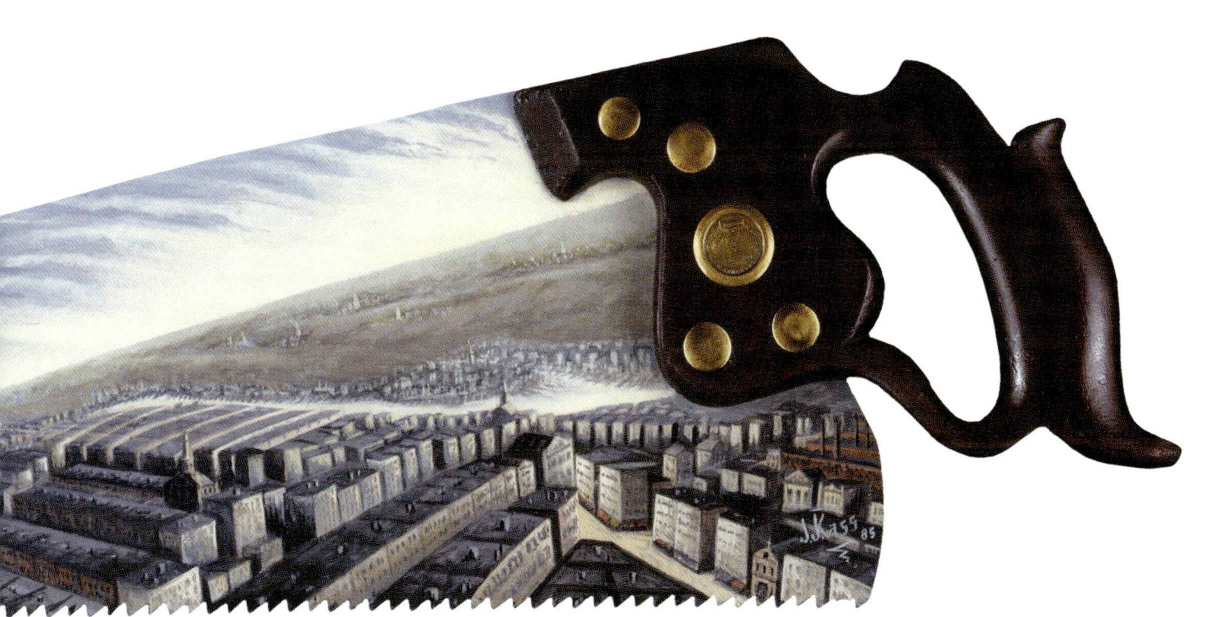

THE VEGATABLE [*sic*] STORE

1986
Magna acrylic and oil on
circular saw
27 in. diam.
Collection of Dr. and
Mrs. Robert Carroll, West
Yarmouth, Massachusetts

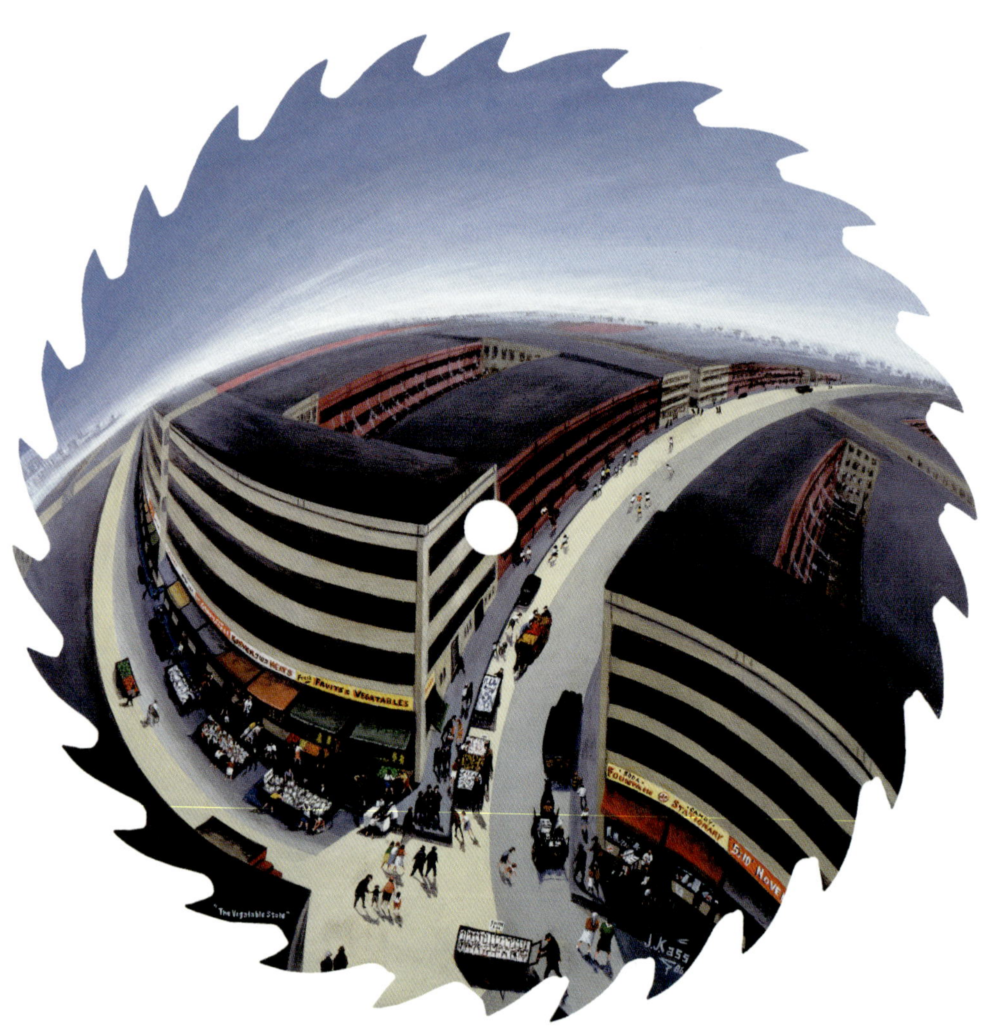

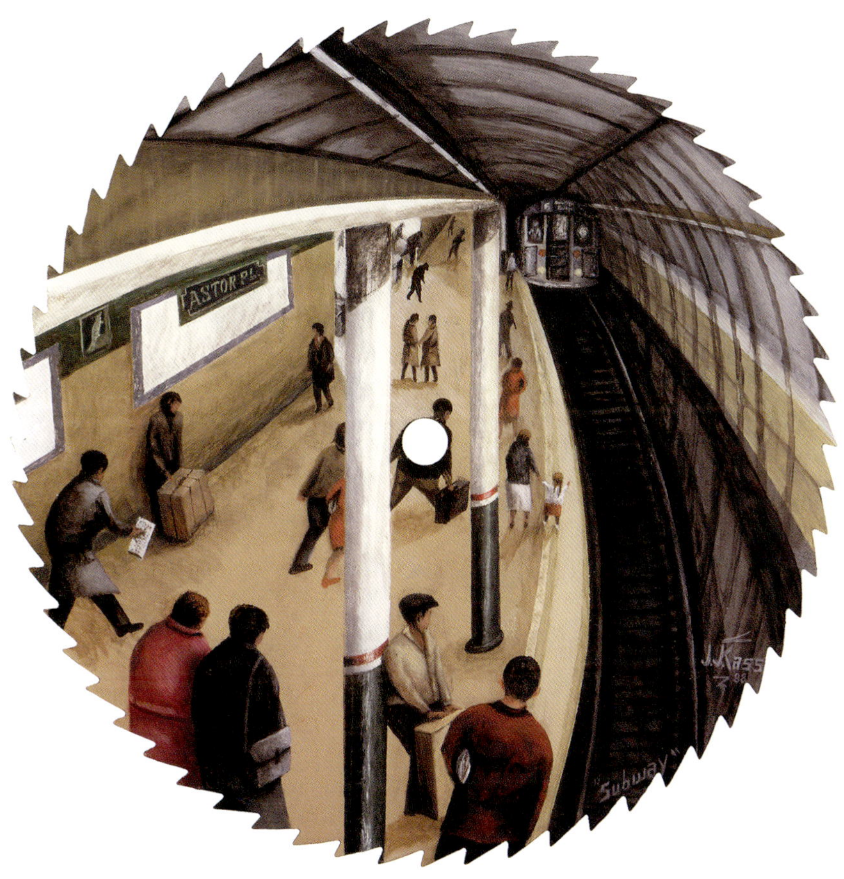

SUBWAY

1988
Magna acrylic and oil on circular saw
18 in. diam.
Collection of Michael and Marilyn Mennello,
Winter Park, Florida

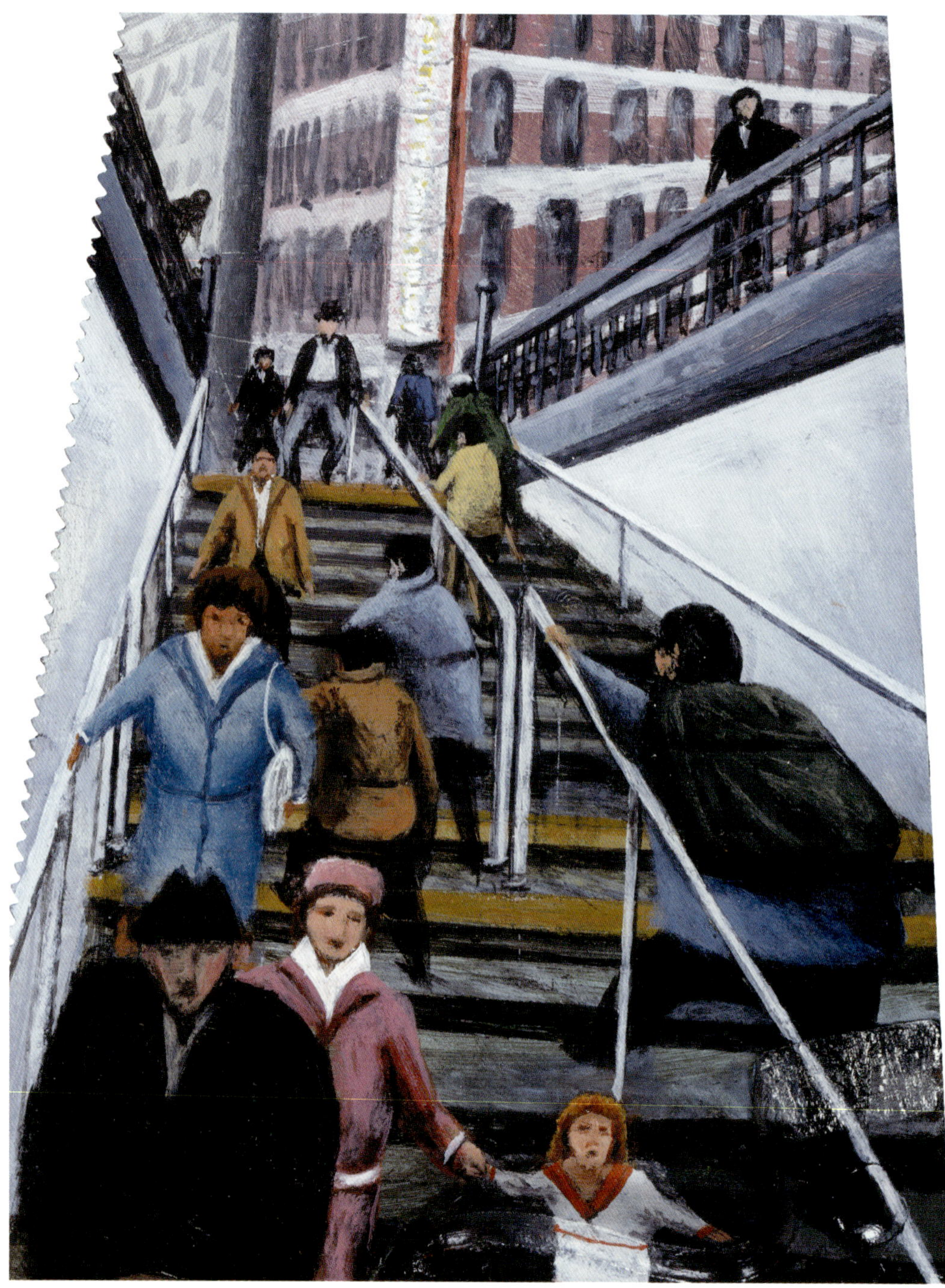

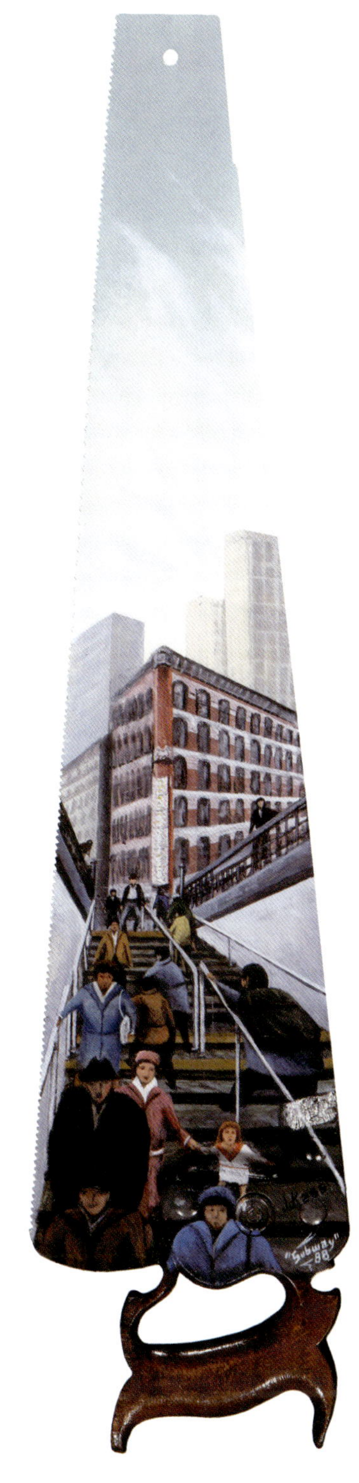

SUBWAY

1988
Magna acrylic and oil on handsaw
30½ × 7 in.
Private collection

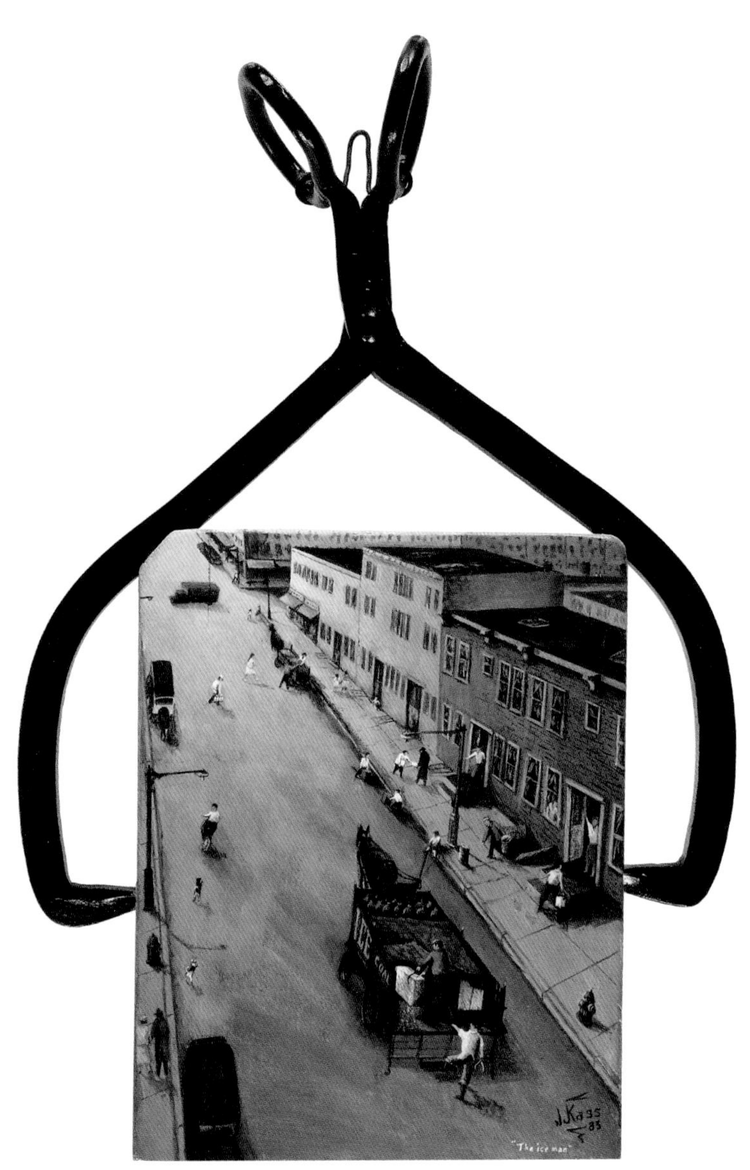

THE ICE MAN

1983
Magna acrylic and oil on wood
panel with ice tongs
20¼ × 14 in.
Private collection

EXHIBITION CHECKLIST

organized by date

PAINTINGS

All paintings are Magna acrylic and oil unless otherwise stated.

Theresa "Rose" Baier Kass Farm in Tachauer Schmettel, Bohemia, 1926
Oil on wood panel, 16 × 20 in.
Private collection
Page 16

Hay Rake in My Meadow, 1979
Handsaw, 6 × 29 in.
Public Art Collection, City of Orlando, Florida

Logging, 1979
Two-man crosscut saw, 7¾ × 40¾ in.
Collection of Courtney Ross-Holst, New York

Moonlight in Vermont #1, 1979
Handsaw, 5¼ × 17½ in.
American Folk Art Museum, gift of Ray Kass and Jerrie Pike, 1999.2.2

Moonlight Skating #2, 1979
Handsaw, 5½ × 22 in.
Collection of Janet Fish, New York

Time to Rest, 1979
Handsaw, 7 × 29 in.
Collection of Rosalind Jacobs, New York

Two Horses in the Meadow, 1979
Back saw, 6 × 14 in.
American Folk Art Museum, gift of Ray Kass and Jerrie Pike, 1999.2.5

Chelsea Sawmill, 1980
Half-section circular saw; forged iron armature by Steven Bickley, 24 × 43 × 5 in.
Private collection
Cover (detail), page 23

The Ox Pull, 1980
Two-handled saw, 7 × 53 in.
Private collection

Sawmill, 1980
Circular saw, 14 in. diam.
Collection of Donald Kuspit, New York

Untitled (Hay Knife), 1980
Hay knife, 5½ × 37 in.
Collection of Nancy Hoffman, New York
Pages 24–25

Untitled (Picking Apples), 1980
Handsaw, 5 × 19 in.
Collection of Sique Spence, New York

Corn Cutters #1, 1981
Corn cutter, 16½ × 11¼ in.
Collection of Richard and Ruth Shack, Miami, Florida
Page 22

My Sugar House Workshop, 1981
Wood panel mounted in bucksaw, 24 × 36 in.
Private collection
Pages 2 (detail), 26

Reflections, 1981
Keyhole saw, 3½ × 13¼ in.
Collection of Susan Shatter,
New York

The Stream, 1981
Pruning saw, 5⅜ × 21 in.
Private collection

Titicus Road, N. Salem, N.Y., 1981
Handsaw, 7½ × 30½ in.
Collection of Allan Stone,
Purchase, New York

The Abandoned Station, 1982
Wood panel mounted in hacksaw,
6 × 28 in.
Collection of Nancy Hoffman
Gallery, New York
Pages 30–31

Back to the Barn, 1982
Grass sickle, 7½ × 17 in.
Private collection
Pages 32–33

Knifing Out a Section of Hay, 1982
Shingle cutter, 14 × 23 in.
Private collection

Moonlight in Vermont #5, 1982
Wood panel mounted in bucksaw,
26 × 33 in.
Collection of Frank Symons, Miami,
Florida
Page 27

The Wheelwright, 1982
Draw blade, 6 × 20 in.
Collection of Ivan Karp, New York
Page 25

The Final Touches, 1983
Wood panel mounted in hacksaw,
6½ × 21 in.
Private collection

The Ice Man, 1983
Wood panel with ice tongs,
20¼ × 14 in.
Private collection
Page 48

Loading the Corn Crib #4, 1983
Corn cutter, 2 × 13 in.
Private collection

Moving Day, 1983
Handsaw, 6¾ × 29 in.
American Folk Art Museum, gift of
Ray Kass and Jerrie Pike, 1999.2.6
Pages 28–29

The Neighborhood, 1983
Handsaw, 6¾ × 29¾ in.
Collection of Richard and Ruth
Shack, Miami, Florida

Pushcarts, 1983
Handsaw, 7 × 29 in.
Collection of Henry and Carol
Goldberg, Chevy Chase, Maryland

Pushcarts, 1983
Handsaw, 7 × 29¾ in.
American Folk Art Museum, gift of
Ray Kass and Jerrie Pike, 1999.2.7
Pages 34–35

Town View, 1983
Handsaw, 6 × 29⅝ in.
American Folk Art Museum, gift of
Ray Kass and Jerrie Pike, 1999.2.3

Pushcarts, 1984
Handsaw, 4¼ × 23½ in.
Collection of Richard and Ruth
Shack, Miami, Florida

Saturday, 1984
Handsaw, 7 × 30½ in.
Estate of Mr. and Mrs. David
McCall, New York

The Catch, 1985
Handsaw, 6¼ × 29½ in.
Tampa Museum of Art, Tampa,
Florida
Pages 30–31

Picking a Team, 1985
Handsaw, 7 × 27½ in.
Estate of Mr. and Mrs. David
McCall, New York
Pages 40–41

Roofs, 1985
Customized handsaw, 7 × 21 in.
American Folk Art Museum, gift of
Ray Kass and Jerrie Pike, 1999.2.4
Pages 42–43

The Vegatable [sic] *Store,* 1986
Circular saw, 27 in. diam.
Collection of Dr. and Mrs. Robert
Carroll, West Yarmouth,
Massachusetts
Page 44

After the Rain, 1987
Handsaw, 5½ × 29½ in.
Collection of Dr. and Mrs. Robert
Carroll, West Yarmouth,
Massachusetts
Pages 36–37

The Alarm, 1987
Handsaw, 7 × 30⅜ in.
Collection of Thurston Twigg-Smith,
Honolulu
Pages 36–37

The Paper Stand, 1987
Handsaw, 6¾ × 28¾ in.
Collection of Lowell Schindler,
courtesy Nancy Hoffman Gallery,
New York
Pages 40–41

Spring Thaw, 1987
Wood panel mounted in child's
bucksaw with wood stand,
21 × 23 in.
Private collection

Back to the Barn #3, 1988
Handsaw, 6½ × 29 in.
Private collection

Capture the Fort, 1988
Handsaw, 5½ × 16½ in.
Private collection

Snowball Fight, 1988
Carpenter's square, 7½ × 10⅝ in.
Private collection
Page 39

Sowing the Field, 1988–1991
Circular saw, 20 in. diam.
American Folk Art Museum, gift of
Ray Kass and Jerrie Pike, 1999.2.1

Spring Thaw, 1988
Wood panel mounted in coping saw,
13 × 29 in.
Private collection

Subway, 1988
Circular saw, 18 in. diam.
Collection of Michael and Marilyn
Mennello, Winter Park, Florida
Pages 1, 45

Subway, 1988
Handsaw, 30½ × 7 in.
Private collection
Pages 46 (detail), 47

Choosing Sides, 1989
Wood panel mounted in hacksaw,
11½ × 22 in.
Private collection
Page 38

Fire! Fire!, 1989
Handsaw, 7 × 29 in.
Private collection

The Ice House, 1989
Ice saw, 19 × 71 in.
Private collection

The Ice House, 1989
Ice saw, 20 × 71 in.
Private collection

The Kiddie Ride, 1989
Handsaw, 5¾ × 25 in.
Private collection

Resting, 1989
Carpenter's square, 4⅝ × 7½ in.
Collection of Allan Stone, Purchase,
New York

Subway #3, 1989
Handsaw, 7¼ × 28¾ in.
Private collection

Back to the Barn, 1990
Handsaw, 7 × 29 in.
Art Museum of Western Virginia,
Roanoke, Virginia

The Last of the Ice Cutting, 1990
Ice saw, 6½ × 34¾ in.
Private collection

Subway, 1990
Handsaw, 29 × 6½ in.
Private collection

The Corner Lot, 1991–1992
Handsaw, 7 × 31 in.
American Folk Art Museum, gift of
Ray Kass and Jerrie Pike, 1999.2.8

The Lots, 1992
Wood panel mounted in bucksaw,
16 × 36½ in.
Private collection

The Old Paint Shop, 1992
Handsaw, 6½ × 24 in.
Private collection

DRAWINGS

All drawings are pencil on paper
with tape.

Moonlight in Vermont #1, 1979
5¼ × 17½ in.
American Folk Art Museum, gift of
Ray Kass and Jerrie Pike, 2001.31.1

Chelsea Sawmill, 1980
17¾ × 41½ in.
Private collection

The Ox Pull, 1980
7 × 53 in.
Private collection

Moving Day #1, 1982
6½ × 27 in.
Private collection

Moving Day #2, 1982
6¼ × 26¼ in.
Private collection
Page 29

Livestock Auction, 1983
10¼ × 27¼ in.
Private collection

The Neighborhood, 1983
6 × 25¼ in.
Private collection

Pushcarts, 1983
6 × 26¾ in.
Private collection
Pages 34–35

Town View, 1983
6 × 29⅝ in.
American Folk Art Museum, gift of
Ray Kass and Jerrie Pike, 2001.31.3

Pushcarts, 1984
6¼ × 26⅛ in.
Private collection

Roofs, 1985
6¼ × 17¾ in.
Private collection
Page 42

Fire! Fire!, 1987
6¼ × 25¾ in.
Private collection

Newspaper Boys, 1987
6¼ × 26 in.
Private collection

Sowing the Field, 1988–1991
20 in. diam.
American Folk Art Museum, gift of
Ray Kass and Jerrie Pike, 2001.31.2

Subway, 1988
18 in. diam.
Private collection

The Ice House, 1989
7 × 54 in.
Private collection

The Ice House, 1989
7 × 54 in.
Private collection

Subway #3, 1989
6 × 25¼ in.
Private collection

The Old Paint Shop, 1992
6 × 20 in.
Private collection

SELECT BIBLIOGRAPHY

de Larminat, Max-Henri. *Objets en dérive*. Paris, France: Centre Georges Pompidou in association with Dessain et Tolra, 1984.

Federal Reserve Board. *Folk Art Traditions: Three Contemporary Masters*. Washington, D.C.: Board of Governors of the Federal Reserve, 1990.

————. *In Celebration of Twenty Years of Collecting Art at the Federal Reserve Board*. Washington, D.C.: Board of Governors of the Federal Reserve, 1996.

Gordon, Peter H., ed. *Diamonds Are Forever: Artists and Writers on Baseball*. San Francisco: Chronicle Books, 1987.

Hamill, Pete. *Tools as Art: The Hechinger Collection*. New York: Harry N. Abrams, 1995.

Lowe Art Museum. *Jacob J. Kass: Painted Saws*. Coral Gables, Fla.: University of Miami, 1982.

Lynes, Russell, William H. Gerdts, and Donald Kuspit. *At the Water's Edge: Nineteenth- and Twentieth-Century American Beach Scenes*. Tampa, Fla.: Tampa Museum of Art, 1989.

Meade, Judson. "Art on Saws." *Americana* 11, no. 1 (March/April 1983): 104.

Mennello Museum of American Folk Art. *Saws, Sickles, Squares, and Tongs: Paintings by Jacob J. Kass*. Orlando, Fla.: Mennello Museum of American Folk Art, 1999.

Pike, Jerrie. "The Painted Saws of Jacob Kass." *Folk Art Messenger* 5, no. 2 (winter 1992): 4–5.

Solomon, Holly, and Alexandra Anderson. *Living With Art*. New York: Rizzoli, 1988, p. 35.

Wolff, Theodor F. "The Many Masks of Modern Art." *Christian Science Monitor* (June 9, 1983): 20.

Yau, John. "Ray and Jacob Kass at Allan Stone." *Art in America* 69, no. 6 (summer 1981): 130–131.

ACKNOWLEDGMENTS

My first thanks are directed to my mentor and friend Gerard C. Wertkin, director of the American Folk Art Museum, who introduced me to the artworks of Jacob J. Kass and to the exhibition project. Enormous appreciation goes to Raymond Kass, whose selfless dedication and unstinting advocacy for recognition of his father's work are both rare and inspiring. Ray participated in many aspects of the project.

Gratitude is offered to the many people who facilitated the exhibition, generously providing information and technical assistance: Johnny Berg, sign painter, Eugene, Ore.; Robert and Ola Habacker; Nancy Hoffman and Sique Spence, Nancy Hoffman Gallery, New York; Bo Joseph, Allan Stone Gallery, New York; Warren Kass; Mark Kissling, archivist, *Signs of the Times;* Andrew Liss; Jerrie Pike; Larry Scheef, archivist, American Truck Historical Society, Kansas City, Mo.; Fuyu Shiraishi; Todd Swanstead; Francis Thompson; Laura Tilden; and Virginia Tech Media Services, Blacksburg, Va.

I am indebted to the following American Folk Art Museum
colleagues who were encouraging throughout the exhibition
preparation and helpful in every way: Cheryl Aldridge, Brooke
Davis Anderson, Benjamin J. Boyington, Janey Fire, Susan
Flamm, Rosemary Gabriel, Tanya Heinrich, Stacy C. Hollander,
Ann-Marie Reilly, Diana Schlesinger, and Judith Gluck Stein-
berg. Thanks also go to Ed Marquand, John Hubbard, and
Marie Weiler at Marquand Books in Seattle.

Finally, thanks to all the lenders who have so willingly
contributed their artworks to the exhibition: Art Museum of
Western Virginia, Roanoke, Va.; Dr. and Mrs. Robert Carroll;
Janet Fish; Henry and Carol Goldberg; Rosalind Jacobs; Ivan
Karp, OK Harris Gallery, New York; Donald Kuspit; Estate of
Mr. and Mrs. David McCall; Michael and Marilyn Mennello;
Nancy Hoffman Gallery, New York; Public Art Collection,
City of Orlando, Fla.; Courtney Ross-Holst; Lowell Schindler;
Richard and Ruth Shack; Susan Shatter; Sique Spence; Allan
Stone, Allan Stone Gallery, New York; Frank Symons; Tampa
Museum of Art, Tampa, Fla.; and Thurston Twigg-Smith.

—L.K.

Published in conjunction with the exhibition "Painted Saws: Jacob Kass," presented at the American Folk Art Museum's Eva and Morris Feld Gallery, New York, July 20–December 1, 2002

10 9 8 7 6 5 4 3 2 1

Library of Congress Control Number: 2002103047
ISBN: 0-912161-15-9

Cover: *Chelsea Sawmill* (detail), 1980 (p. 23)
Page 1: *Subway,* 1988 (p. 45)
Page 2: *My Sugar House Workshop* (detail), 1981 (p. 26)

Photography credits: Courtesy Robert Habacker, p. 9; Ray Kass, pp. 4, 7, 18; Courtesy Kass family archives, p. 12; Virginia Tech Media Services, Blacksburg, Va., pp. 16, 22–48

Edited by Tanya Heinrich
Designed by John Hubbard
Color separations by iocolor, Seattle
Produced by Marquand Books, Inc., Seattle
   www.marquand.com
Printed by C & C Offset Printing Co., Ltd., Hong Kong